EDMUND LUDLOW AND THE ENGLISH CIVIL WAR

HEINEMANN
HISTORY EYEWITNESS

EDITED WITH AN INTRODUCTION
AND ADDITIONAL MATERIAL BY
JANE SHUTER

Heinemann

Published by Heinemann Library,
an imprint of Heinemann Publishers (Oxford) Ltd,
Halley Court, Jordan Hill, Oxford OX2 8EJ

OXFORD LONDON EDINBURGH MADRID
ATHENS BOLOGNA PARIS MELBOURNE
SYDNEY AUCKLAND SINGAPORE TOKYO
IBADAN NAIROBI HARARE GABORONE
PORTSMOUTH NH (USA)

Selection and additional material
© Heinemann Publishers (Oxford) Ltd 1994

First published 1994
This edition 1995
All rights reserved: no part of this publication may be reproduced, stored in a retrieval system, or transmitted in any form or by any means, electronic, mechanical, photocopying, recording, or otherwise, without the written permission of the Publishers.

99 98 97 96 95
10 9 8 7 6 5 4 3 2 1

British Library Cataloguing in Publication Data
Edmund Ludlow and the English Civil War. –
(History Eyewitness Series)
I. Shuter, Jane II. Series
942.062092

ISBN 0 431 07161 6

Designed by Green Door Design Ltd., map by Jeff Edwards
Printed in China

Acknowledgements
The publishers would like to thank the following for permission to reproduce photographs:

Ashmolean Museum: pp.14, 23, 31, 34
Avxiu Mas: p.27
Bridgeman Art Library: p.42
British Library Reproductions: pp.24, 39
C. M. Dixon: pp.10, 12
Duke of Buccleuch: p.40
English Heritage Photographic Library: pp.17, 18, 19, 21
Fotomas Index: pp.13, 15
Hulton Deutsch Collection: p.32
Mansell Collection: p.6
National Galleries of Scotland: cover and p.37
National Portrait Gallery: pp.7, 8, 45
Royal Armouries, Tower of London: p.28

The cover photograph shows the execution of Charles I.

Every effort has been made to contact copyright holders of material reproduced in this book. Any omissions will be rectified in subsequent printings if notice is given to the publisher.

Note to the reader

In this book some of the words are printed in **bold** type. This indicates that the word is listed in the glossary on pages 46–7. The glossary gives a brief explanation of words that may be new to you.

CONTENTS

Introduction		4
Chapter 1	Taking Sides	6
Chapter 2	Early Fighting	8
Chapter 3	The Siege of Wardour Castle	16
Chapter 4	A Prisoner!	22
Chapter 5	Fighting in 1644	24
Chapter 6	Parliament and the Army	30
Chapter 7	The Second Civil War	32
Chapter 8	Trial and Execution of the King	34
Chapter 9	England without a King	38
Chapter 10	Monarchy Restored	42
Chapter 11	Royalist Revenge	44
Glossary		46
Index		48

Introduction

The English Civil War
The English Civil War was in fact three wars:
- **The First Civil War, 1642–6** which ended with the surrender of Charles I.
- **The Second Civil War, 1648** which ended with the defeat of the Scots at Preston.
- **The Third Civil War, 1651** led by Charles I's son (Charles I was executed in 1649) and which ended with his defeat at Worcester.

There were almost as many reasons for people to fight the Civil War as there were people fighting. Briefly, however, the main reason for the war was that King Charles I and his various parliaments did not agree about anything – religion, how the country should be run, how England should behave towards other countries and so on. This was made worse by the fact that Charles I, believing that kings got their power from God and so could rule as they chose, made no attempt to keep his parliaments happy. He spent eleven years ruling without parliaments at all. When the Long Parliament, called in 1640, tried to make him change his ways and he refused, war broke out.

Edmund Ludlow, 1617? –1692
Ludlow was the son of a country gentleman. He went to grammar school, university (Trinity College, Oxford) and the Inns of Court in London (where young gentlemen learned the law). He married, but tells us little about his wife and does not seem to have had children. Ludlow was a great supporter of the law, and this is one reason why he sided with Parliament in the Civil Wars and why he fell out with the army when it tried to rule by the sword. He was a very religious person. He was a Puritan and believed that God took a hand in matters on earth, guiding people by providence. He also believed in doing his duty which, according to his memoirs, led him to taking on several jobs for his country that he would have preferred to have refused.

Ludlow's views and this account
Ludlow's account of the English Revolution is affected by his political and religious beliefs. He is far from unbiased, especially in his views about Cromwell and the army after 1650.

This account has concentrated on events that Ludlow experienced first hand, except where a certain amount of narrative is necessary to give a framework. This means that the account does not deal with the wars that were fought with the Dutch and in the West Indies at this time, nor does it deal with any of the 'big' battles of the Civil Wars except for Edgehill, which Ludlow was directly involved in.

This map shows the main places that Ludlow mentions in his story.

Chapter 1

Taking Sides

I thought it my duty as an Englishman to serve my country in the army of Parliament commanded by the Earl of Essex. The justice of our cause seemed clear to me. I thought there would be some foreigners who the King had brought to court who would side with him, as well as the clergy he had so promoted. Yet I could not believe that many of the people, long oppressed with many burdens by the King, would support him. They had an elected Parliament, got after long difficulty, which was prepared to fight for their rights. So it seemed unlikely to me that there would be many people who would be so treacherous and unworthy as to strengthen the hand of the enemy against those who had God and the law on their side.

So I met with Mr Richard Fiennes and Mr Charles Fleetwood who were studying law at the Inns of Court with me. We decided to gather together as many young men from the Inns of Court as we could, and to learn how to fight, in case we should be needed.

We found someone who was experienced in military affairs to instuct us in the use of arms, and for some time we frequently met to train at the Artillery Ground in London. We then heard that Parliament was to raise a life-guard for the Earl of Essex, to consist of a hundred gentlemen commanded by Sir Philip Stapleton, MP. Most of our company decided to join, and we were so many that we made up the greater part of the group.

This print, made in 1642, shows the artist's view of the beginnings of taking sides in the First Civil War. Charles I and his supporters, called Royalists, are shown on the left, with a poodle. The supporters of Parliament, called Parliamentarians, are on on the right, with their dog. The insults that the dogs are swapping are one of the earliest uses of the names 'Roundhead' and 'Cavalier'. They were used, in the way the dogs are using them, as insults.

A painting of Charles I dictating a message to one of his secretaries, Edward Walker. At the time, secretaries were men, never women. Reading and writing was a skill that far fewer people had then, and such work was not considered women's work. Secretaries wrote letters, arranged business affairs and generally organized the lives of their employers. Walker is using a pen set that packed away into a steel tube, so that it would not get damaged while being carried about.

Walker is writing on a drum, using it as a sort of table. This is the kind of drum that would have been used in battle. Walker is wearing a buff coat (a thick leather coat) that was worn in battle because it was flexible, strong and not as heavy as armour. Charles I is wearing some armour, a covering for the chest and back called a 'back and breast'. Both Walker and King Charles are armed with swords and wearing long leather boots called 'bucket boots'. The King may have worn the helmet behind him into battle, but it would have been very heavy. It is more likely that it was 'dress armour', just for show. Charles I is holding a short pole to show that he is in command of the army.

CHARLES I

Charles I believed that kings got their power directly from God and could rule without Parliament – or anyone else – interfering. However, MPs at this time wanted more say in how the country was run, not less.

Other monarchs had tried to keep on the right side of Parliament, but Charles I met the MPs head on. He told them bluntly they had no right to tell him what to do. When he was forced to agree to changes, through his need for money which only Parliament could grant, he went back on his word as soon as he could, if possible. He was even prepared to resort to civil war rather than to give in to the demands of the MPs.

It seemed that the people, hoping that this was the time for them to free themselves from the oppression of the King, readily offered themselves to serve in the army of Parliament. So it was not long before the army, under the command of the Earl of Essex, was raised, and ready to march.

At first it seemed as though I had been right about the lack of support for the King. He mananged to raise very little support while he was in York. Things changed, however, when he and his people moved on to Shrewsbury, for here he was joined by many people from Wales and the nearby counties.

CHAPTER 2

Early Fighting

*A seventeenth century painting which shows a civil war **musketeer** standing outside a tent, with a battle going on in the background, and armour and weapons heaped up in the foreground. There is a cannon on the left, with pikes, muskets, armour standards [flags] and even a drum. Standards were important, especially at the start of the war, because they clearly showed whose side people were on. For much of the First Civil War it was very hard to tell the sides apart in battle, for they wore much the same clothes, and had similar weapons. Things could get very confused.*

The Battle of Powicke Bridge

The Earl of Essex was brought the news that the King and his army were marching towards Worcester, so we advanced there too. As we approached we were told that Prince Rupert had taken the town for the King, and that a party of ours, impatient of delay, had **engaged** the enemy before we could arrive. Our men had had some thousand **horse** and **dragoons**, the enemy outnumbered them. They met beyond a bridge between Pershore and Worcester. Our men decided to cross the bridge and attack. Not more than half of them were across – for they could not advance more than eight or ten at a time due to the lane on the other side being narrow – when the enemy attacked them. They were forced to retreat, and this they did in great disorder, as you can imagine from the fact of their disadvantageous position. Some were killed, including Major Gunter, who had tried to dissuade them from the attack in the first place. Others were drowned, others were taken prisoner, including Colonel Sands who led the **party**. The prisoners were taken into Worcester, where Sands later died of his wounds. The rest of our **routed** men returned in great disorder to Pershore.

Pershore was where our life-guard were **quartered** that night. So, as we marched into the town we were met by horsemen riding very hard towards us with drawn swords, many of them without their hats. They told us of Parliament's loss, a tale much exaggerated by their fears and excitements. They told us that the enemy was in hard pursuit of them, and likely to arrive in the town at any moment, whereas it later appeared that they had not come within four miles of Pershore. But we did not realize how unlikely their tale was. As we were as yet strangers to battle we were much alarmed by this report, yet some of us (unwilling to believe everything until we were better informed) offered to go to investigate the truth of the matter.

Our captain, Sir Philip Stapleton, was not with us, so we were being led by his lieutenant, an old soldier called Bainham. He gathered us together in a field outside the town, where he said we would be well placed to engage the enemy. He commanded us to '**wheel about**' to be ready to face the enemy should they arrive. But our gentlemen seemed to not understand the difference between 'wheel about' and 'shift for yourselves' as commands. Fearing the enemy to be close, they fled back to the army and the town in a very dishonourable manner.

Next morning the life-guard assembled at headquarters. We received a cold welcome from the general, which, it must be said, we well deserved after our actions of the previous day. The next night the enemy left Worcester, and retreated to Shrewsbury, which the King and his main army had never left. The Earl of Essex then entered Worcester, and set up his headquarters there. A message was sent to the King, asking him to return to London to talk with Parliament, and we waited at Worcester for an answer. The King used the time of waiting to build up his army, for he had no notion of abandoning the fight at this time.

Once the King had gathered as many men as he could, his army began to march. The Earl of Essex followed after him with the Parliamentary army. The Earl sent **scouts** to watch their movements. So for some two days we followed them. Then, on the morning of Sunday, 23 October, 1642, our scouts brought news, at about nine o'clock in the morning, that the enemy were at Edgehill, in Warwickshire. On hearing this, our forces, who had been sent to get some rest, having been on the march with little rest for the past forty-eight hours, were told to get ready to engage with the enemy.

READY FOR WAR?

England had not taken part in a major land war for over 100 years. Most men should have had some military training in the **militia**. However, the militia was not taken very seriously. In many parts of the country the one day each year spent training the militia was more like a fair, with sideshows, and with many of the men supposed to be training getting drunk instead. So there were very few men in England who knew much about being a soldier before the Civil War started. Some, like Bainham who Ludlow mentions, had fought in the wars in Europe. At the start of the war these men, with their experience, were very important. As the war continued soldiers like Ludlow, or Cromwell, who learned all they knew fighting in England, became more important.

The Battle of Edgehill

The enemy drew down the hill, and we assembled in a field near Keinton. The best of our **field pieces** were on our right **wing**, guarded by two regiments of **foot** and some horse. Our general commanded the gunners to fire on the enemy, in that part of their army where, as it was reported, the King was. This they did twice. The great shot was exchanged on both sides for the space of an hour, or thereabouts. Then the foot began to engage, and a party of the enemy was sent to line some hedges on our right wing to beat us from the battleground. But their plan failed, they were driven off by our dragoons, without any loss on our side.

The enemy's **body** of foot, where the King's **standard** was, came to within a **musket**-shot of us. When we saw they were this close, and that there were no horsemen from their side within reach to stop us, we charged them. Some of our men were killed by their **pikemen**, but no one was harmed by their muskets. We could not break their ranks, so we retreated to our former position.

No sooner had we arrived than we saw that the soldiers who were supposed to be guarding the **artillery** were marching off. Sir Philip Stapleton, our captain, thought the guns should not be left unguarded, so we promised to defend them.

This civil war soldier, and the one on page 12, are part of a stained glass window in the Church of St Chad, Farndon. The window was made in 1660 to remember Royalists who fought in the siege of Chester. Chester was one of the last places to hold out for Charles I, despite suburbs being burned, famine and sickness. It was forced to surrender on 3 February, 1646.

This man on is probably a captain. He is holding a partisan (a short spear) in his right hand. Partisans were usually only carried by captains.

The sash around his waist would have been a particular colour to show which side he supported.

We sent one of our servants to load and level one of the guns. He had only just done this when a body of horse appeared, advancing towards us from the enemy's side of the field. We fired at them with **case-shot**, but did little damage, only wounding one man through the hand, because our **gun** was overloaded, and on too high a piece of ground to get a good aim.

It was just as well we did not do further damage, for the body of horse came from our own side, commanded by Sir William Balfour, who had charged right into the enemy ranks with great resolution to **nail** several of their cannon. The horse were returning to our own party. The man who was shot in the hand was giving us notice of what side he was on by holding his hand up; but unfortunately we did not understand that this was his meaning. The Earl of Essex now ordered two regiments of foot to attack the body of men that we had charged before, where the King's standard was. This they did, but they could not break through the enemy ranks until Sir William Balfour led a party of horse to charge them at the rear. Then our horse attacked to the side at the same time, so they broke, and ran away towards the hill.

Many of the Royalists were killed here, among them Sir Edward Varney, the King's standard-bearer, who joined the fight on the King's side more out of duty than out of conviction. The King's standard was taken by our side, I saw it displayed by Lieutenant Colonel Middleton. He took it to the Earl of Essex, who put it into the care of his secretary, Mr Chambers. Then a Captain Smith, from the other side, with two more from his side, all disguised with orange coloured scarves (the Earl of Essex's **colour**) came to Chambers and said that it was not fit that someone who was not a soldier should carry it. They took the standard from him, and rode back to the King with it, for which, I hear, he was knighted.

Now my party was forced to retreat by a party of horse; we did not want to have our standard taken. In the confusion, as I was making my way back to our army, I fell in with some soldiers that I soon realized were a body of the King's foot. I was lucky enough to pass through them without them discovering the side I was on. I then met with Sir William Balfour's troop, some of whom did not know me, and were about to fire on me, taking me for one of the enemy.

Luckily they were prevented, and assured to the contrary, by one Mr Francis Russell, who knew me, because he was a member of our life-guard. He had joined with ten men, all well mounted and armed. He paid for the keep of these men and their equipment, and even their horses, himself. He had also got separated from the army, and his men, in the heat of the pursuit.

CONFUSION ON THE BATTLEFIELD

The image which many people have of the Royalist fighting in satin and lace, while the Parliamentarians wore black is wrong. Most people were similarly dressed and armed, no matter what side they were on. This could, and did, lead to confusion, especially early in the war.

Both sides tried to avoid the confusion. They tried wearing sashes of certain colours – but this could be used to the enemy's advantage, as it was to recapture the King's standard. They tried passwords – but these could be overheard, or even guessed at, the Royalist password at Edgehill, for instance, was 'For God and King Charles'. They tried wearing leaves from certain trees, or even pieces of paper, in their hats – but these were easily lost or not noticed in the heat of battle.

In an age when even the most famous people were not known by sight it was easy to avoid detection. Charles I once escaped from Oxford by putting on simple clothes and walking straight out, pretending to be someone's servant.

A musketeer from the same church window as the soldier on page 10. Again, even though he is a Royalist musketeer, the Parliamentarians would have looked similar. Slung around his body is a leather strap. The things hanging from the strap are wooden containers that hold one bullet and enough gunpowder to fire it.

We were now in a lull in the battle, except for a few of the enemy's great guns which continued to fire on us. Towards the close of day we discovered a party of horse coming from our rear on the left of us, under the hedges. The life-guard (which I had by then found), having made sure that they were indeed the enemy, resolved to charge them. They sent a message to some of our troops, but a musket-shot away, asking them to come up to support us. Despite their refusal to help us, and that the only way of reaching the enemy was through a small gap in the hedge, we decided to try. We advanced towards them, and fell upon their rear. We killed several of them, and managed to capture some of their weapons. While we were doing this I fell off my horse, and could not, without great difficulty, get back on again, as I was now, like the rest, loaded down with the enemy's weapons.

We later discovered that the group we had attacked were part of the right wing of the King's horse, which was commanded by Prince Rupert. The reason for them being so far in our camp fell out in this way. Our own horse had put our footsoldiers into disorder, for the footsoldiers had had to open their ranks to give our horse a passage to retreat from the King's horse. Prince Rupert, seeing the break in our ranks, pressed upon our men with such fury that they broke ranks and ran away. Here he allowed greed to outweigh tactics. For he spent too much time pursuing our men too far, and plundering the wagons of provisions and other stuff behind our lines. Had this time been used by him to take advantage of the disarray on the battlefield, where the fight was, he might have helped to bring off a victory for his side.

The night after the battle our army quartered on the same ground that the enemy had fought on the day before. No man got any meat [food] that night, nor the horses either. I myself had had no meat since the Saturday before. Nor was this all to give me discomfort. Because of all the coming and going, I could not find my servant, who had my cloak. So, having nothing to keep me warm but a suit of iron, I was forced to walk up and down all night, to try to keep warm. The night itself was very cold, because there was a sharp frost. Towards morning our army was joined by Colonel Hampden's and other regiments, about 4,000 men, who had not been able to get to us sooner. About daylight, we saw the enemy on the hill, and judged they would not attack again. We were able to go and bury our dead, and theirs too if we saw fit to do so. The day was spent sending trumpeters from one side to another, asking if those who were missing on both sides were dead or prisoners. The greatest slaughter on our side was of those who ran away. On the other side it was of those who had stood firm. Some sixty men lay dead where the King's standard was taken. That night we were provided with food. We were glad of it, yet when I got some meat I could hardly eat it. I seemed almost to be unable to move my jaws, for want of use.

The Storming of Brentford

Our army was now refreshed, and masters of the field. We had now more men, so hoped to pursue the enemy, who were marching off as fast as they could. Instead, for reasons I do not know, we marched to Warwick. Prince Rupert, hearing of our leaving, fell on the town of Kineton, where our sick and wounded soldiers lay, cruelly murdered many of them and then returned to the King's army. The King marched to Oxford. From Warwick our army returned to London. Parliament now sent messages to the King, saying that they wished to avoid more bloodshed, and come to terms. The King's answer suggested that he wished for peace too. Parliament believed the message, but the very next day the King took advantage of a very thick mist to march his army to within half a mile of Brentford, intending to attack our artillery (which was at Hammersmith), the Parliament and the City. He would have succeeded, had not he been discovered.

Two regiments of foot and a small party of horse, which happened to be quartered in Brentford, then opposed his passage, hoping to hold out until more troops could come to their aid. They held out, with unspeakable courage, and stopped the march of the King's army for most of the afternoon. They were quite surrounded by horse and foot, overpowered in numbers on all sides, and many brave and gallant men were killed. When it was obviously hopeless, the rest of the men chose to leap into the river and risk drowning, rather than surrender. Many officers and soldiers were drowned, and some were caught and taken prisoner. During this time those units of our army that were quartered around London drew together. Our life-guard were quicker than most, for we had been assembled in Chelsea Fields to **muster**, when we heard the shooting as it was taking place at Brentford. The enemy, having lost the element of surprise, were discouraged from advancing any further that night.

> **MASTERS OF THE FIELD?**
> Ludlow says that the Parliamentary army were 'masters of the field'. There are also accounts of the battle from the Royalist side that claim they were the winners. But, in reality, no one really won. The fighting just stopped when it was too dark to fight any longer and did not start again. Battles and skirmishes often ended in this inconclusive way.

A picture of the battle of Edgehill, taken from the front one of the many weekly newsbooks sold during the Civil War. They were the first newspapers in this country.

Notice how tall the pikes are that the footsoldiers are carrying. They were very heavy, and difficult to use. The standards are also clearly shown. It is unlikely that the battle would really have looked this tidy. People would not have been this organized.

Battles such as Edgehill, involving many men and 'great guns' and formal fighting were the exception. Skirmishes between smaller groups on each side were much more common, as were sieges of towns or castles.

One of the coins made by the Royalists. This was made in Oxford in 1644. Money was a problem to both sides during the war. In theory both sides paid their soldiers a daily wage. In fact the soldiers were not paid regularly, or even very often. Some commanders, Ludlow was one of them, paid their soldiers with their own money, hoping to be repaid eventually.

Turnham Green

The Parliament was alarmed at the danger and the treachery of this act. They decided to act quickly and by eight of the clock the next morning we had a body of some 20,000 horse and foot drawn up on Turnham Green, a mile this side of Brentford. There were also more of our soldiers marching towards us from Kingston.

A party then drew away from the main body of the enemy force, and tried to move towards Acton. We attacked this smaller party, and it was forced to rejoin the main body. Here, as at Edgehill, we then lost the chance to attack the enemy while we had them outnumbered and at a disadvantage. But the Earl of Holland and others set themselves to dissuade the Earl of Essex from attacking the enemy at this time, magnifying the size of the enemy to him. As he did not press our advantage, he succeeded in giving the enemy time to draw off towards Kingston. This they did as fast as they could, leaving only a small party behind in order to secure their retreat. Towards evening, we were ordered to fire our great guns upon this party. The life-guard were in the roadway, set to stop a charge upon our foot by any of their horse. But the enemy was in a flying, not in a charging condition; no sooner had our cannon opened fire on them than the rearguard retreated to join the main body of the army, which then made its headquarters at Kingston.

Kingston had the advantage of needing to be approached by way of a bridge over the River Thames, this helped to even out the fact that the enemy were outnumbered. So our general had a bridge of boats made across the river, to cancel out their advantage. No sooner had he finished this, than the enemy retreated to Oxford, by way of Reading, which they **garrisoned**. Now was a time when both sides began to garrison the important towns for the winter. The King spent the winter in Oxford. The Parliamentary army spent the winter in Windsor. Parliament again sent messages to the King at this time, asking him to reach a peace, despite his treacherous actions over the last agreement. This time he made no pretence of accepting them. The winter passed peacefully, without much happening at any of the garrisons, with the exception of a Royalist attack on our garison at Henley, which was beaten off.

WINTER
Fighting had always been a seasonal occupation. There came a point when the weather got too bad to fight, and both sides gave up for the winter. Sometimes they would settle down to besiege a town or a castle, at other times, to save money, soldiers were just sent home until the spring, when they were next needed.

Wardour Castle captured from the Royalists

In about March, 1643, Sir Edward Hungerford, having been told to raise and take command of troops for Parliament in Wiltshire, invited me to raise a troop of horse for his regiment. I went to meet him in Devizes, and we went to Salisbury, and took horses and weapons from people suspected of Royalist sympathies there, to arm our own men. I did all I could to raise my own troop, and went back to Windsor to report on what was going on. I returned to Wiltshire in April, with three of the life-guard. Two of them were to become officers in my troop, the third to join another troop in the same regiment. We found Sir Edward Hungerford and Colonel Stroud besieging Wardour Castle. They had been there for about a week, battering it with two small guns, but had done little but put a shot in at a window and destroy a chimney piece. There were tunnels on either side of the castle, which were used to carry away the rubbish and sewage, and so two or three barrels of gunpowder were put into one of them and set light to. This blew up a part of the castle. We then fired our muskets, and the face of one of the servants was grazed by a bullet. These things, with the threat of firing the other tunnel and storming the castle within an hour, so terrified the ladies in the castle that they agreed to surrender it.

Sir Edward entrusted the government of the castle to my care and left me a company of foot commanded by Captain Bean, as well as my own troop, to defend it. I levelled the works that had been raised by our side during the siege, sunk a well, and had the tunnels seen to. I then laid in provisions, for I expected that we would soon be besieged in our turn, as we were soon after. Within a fortnight after I was left in charge, the Lord Arundel, to whom the castle belonged, supposing that I would be as yet unprovided for, came with a party of horse and commanded me to give it to him in the name of the King. Some who were with me advised me to do so, but I replied that I was entrusted to keep the castle for Parliament, and could not surrender it until they ordered me to do so. The enemy were not ready at that time to attack us, so they returned to the main body of their army.

I was soon told that a party of the King's horse were in Salisbury, so I set out with six of my troop to do what I could to pick off enemy stragglers. When I reached Sutton I was told that six of them had gone into the town just before. We made after them, and saw their horses tied up in the yard of a house. I went in, and was no sooner in than the door was shut upon me, but my men rushed the house, and got the door open. The two who had shut me in fled. A third escaped on one of my men's horse. The other three were in an upper room and surrendered on the promise that they would be allowed to live. So we returned to the castle with three prisoners and six horse.

WARDOUR CASTLE

Wardour Castle was the home of the Lord Arundel. When Ludlow arrived at Wardour, Lord Arundel was with the King, at Oxford. The castle was being defended by his wife, Lady Blanche. It was she who surrendered it to Sir Edward Hungerford and Ludlow.

The castle was built in 1393 for Lord Lovell, a six-sided castle, quite small compared to many, with just one defensive wall. It had been changed over the years to make it more of a home and less of a military site. After the Civil Wars it was never repaired.

A picture from the same newsbook as on page 13. It shows the Parliamentarian capture of Wardour Castle from Blanche, Lady Arundel.

Chapter 3

The Siege of Wardour Castle

The enemy were now beginning to close in, yet they did not besiege us until they had tried to take us by treachery. They found a boy of some twelve years of age who was so bad that he had already tried to poison his grandfather. He was sent to the castle to ask for work, which I allowed, not suspecting one so young. A few days later a party of enemy horse appeared making a great noise, which frightened our cattle, about forty cows and a bull, into running away. Some of us went to try to turn the cattle back, and were fired on so fiercely that one of my soldiers and I had to climb a tree for shelter. A ball from an enemy musket hit the tree and was forced downwards, shooting the young man in the hand and me in the leg. The enemy were driven off by the firing of a cannon from the castle. We got back, but I had to keep to my bed for two days. Meanwhile some of the soldiers became suspicious of the boy, and questioned him. He said he had been ill treated for speaking well of Parliament, yet they were not satisfied with his answer. So, to frighten him, they threatened to hang him if he did not tell the truth. So he confessed that he had been hired to spy and report back on the number of men in the garrison. As well as this he was to **poison** the arms, the well and the beer, blow up the ammunition and steal the best of my horses. For this he was to be paid half a crown [12.5p]. He then said he had already poisoned two cannon, but pretended his conscience would not let him poison the beer. The great guns were repaired by oiling them and then lighting a fire in them.

After this we got in some cattle to replace those we had lost. Yet we had not many, and the enemy got into the villages to stop us collecting any more. But one market day we slipped out, went to market, siezed all the provisions there (paying for them, which caused much surprise) and got them back to the castle safe. We were no sooner in than the enemy closed in around the castle. They used a fallen tree to make a safe observation post near the gate of the castle. From here they shot several of my men as they went out to fetch wood. The besiegers were commanded by Captain Bowyer, who offered us **terms** to leave the castle, which we declined. He threatened that great numbers of horse and foot, and several cannon, were on their way. He boasted of the right of his cause and spoke of our danger and inevitable ruin. Captain Bean, our cannoneer, told him were sure of the right of our cause too, and would stay. He fired at Bowyer, and caught him in the heel. He fell to the ground. No one dared fetch him all day. By nightfall his wound had **gangrene** and he died. He was replaced with a Colonel Barnes. My father had found employment with Parliament for Barnes, because he was an experienced soldier. He had stayed as long as the pay lasted, then he joined the King. He set up a fort within musket shot of us, in the hill that surrounded the castle except to the west, where there was a pond.

> **PROVISIONS**
>
> Weapons, armour and ammunition for the war were in short supply. Often capturing an enemy canon (or putting it out of action) was one of the most important action in a skirmish. Ludlow would get such supplies from the nearest big garrison, which would let people have what they could spare.
>
> Food and drink came from the local people. Ludlow says he was always careful to pay for this. There were many people who were far less scrupulous, as complaints from the time make clear.
>
> Horses were another thing in short supply. They were got in several ways – taken from the enemy, provided by their own side, or taken from the local people.

The enemy took over the **outhouses** of the castle, but used them only at night. So we sent some forty men into the outhouses through a secret tunnel, telling them to lie in wait and surprise the enemy. This would have worked, but one of our men fired his pistol too early, frightening them off. A kinsman of mine came to get me to surrender. I let him come in and arranged things so that we seemed well provisioned. I put small barrels inside larger ones, with just a layer of meat or corn on the top to make it seem as if we had far more than we really had. I proposed a limited surrender, but did not expect any reply to my terms, and got none. We now had no beer, only water in the well. Our corn was low and so we rationed it. There were now a hundred men. When our meat ran out we killed and ate one of the captured horses. The enemy then had a lucky shot, which broke the chain of our portcullis, so we could no longer use the gate. We barricaded it up on the inside; now we had no way out but through a window, for we had walled up our other doors earlier.

The enemy now decided to dig a hole in the castle wall to blow the wall up, or to tunnel under it, supporting the tunnel with timber, then light a fire in the tunnel to bring the wall down. They brought up thick oak planks to the walls one dark night, on either side of the castle. Our men found them on one side and beat them off, forcing them to leave the planks behind. They had more luck on the other side, and got the the planks set up to form a shelter. In the morning we heard them digging. We could not trace where the noise of digging was coming from. Then we found them and tried to shift them by pouring down hot water and melted lead, to little effect. We then threw hand grenadoes, and they were forced to go, leaving their tools and provisions. Despite the fact that there was no way out but by a window we managed to get the tools and provisions.

A plan of Wardour Castle and its grounds. The secret passage that Ludlow's men used to reach the outhouses is clearly marked on this plan. The castle was not very well sited, as there was high ground around it which was an advantage to the enemy, not the defenders.

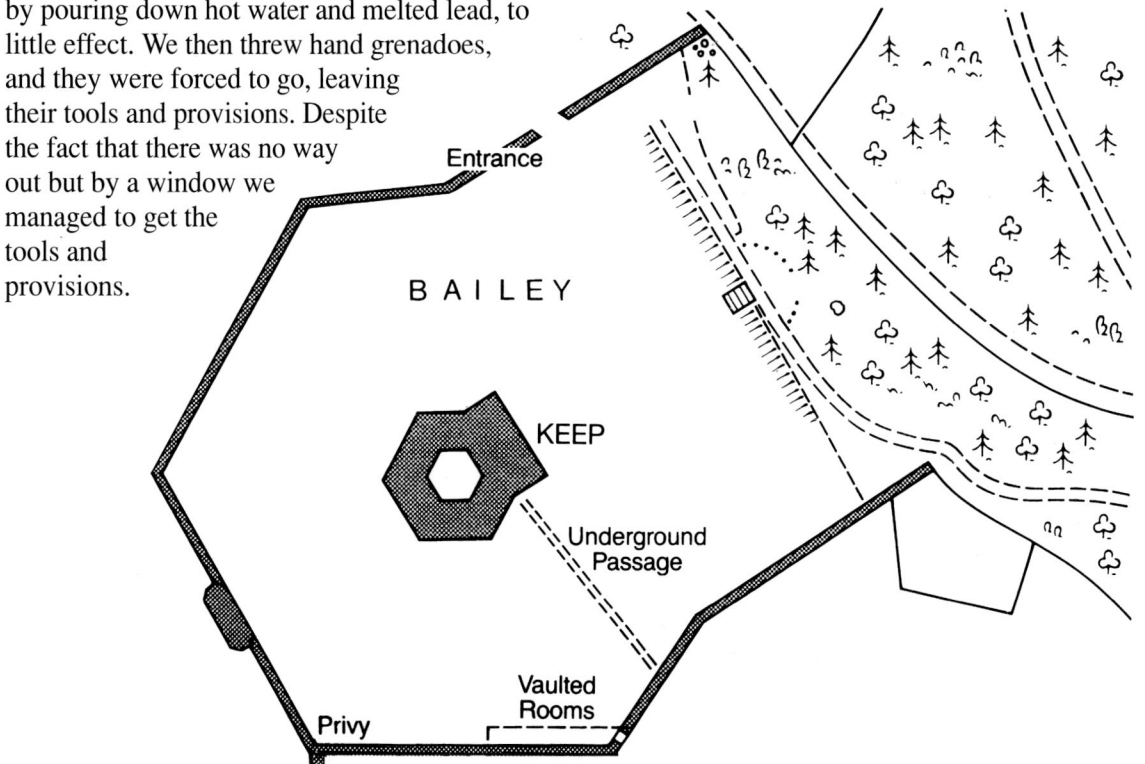

About the middle of January, 1644, Sir William Waller assured that, if we could hold out just another two weeks, he would relieve us, or lay his bones under our walls. The garrisons at Southampton and Poole also offered some hopes of help. I offered them some £700 if they would come, but they did not. My troop of horse were doing what they could to outwit the enemy and help our relief. Now the King sent Sir Francis Doddington with more men to the castle, and among them an engineer to **undermine** the castle. As soon as we heard them beginning to dig, we began to try to undermine them, but the floor was too hard to break through.

We had no medicines and our surgeon had been shot and disabled. One of his brothers decided to go through a window to get him medicine from somewhere. We set up a lot of noise and firing at the other end of the castle to draw the enemy's notice. They got past the guard, and made their way to a friendly house, where they were told that relief would be with us within ten days. But ten days passed and ten more after them. No help came. I was sent a letter by Sir Francis Doddington, reminding me that our families had long been friends, and asking me to surrender the castle before it was too late. I replied that, while I was grateful for his offer, I was holding the castle for Parliament, in whose cause I would gladly lay down my life in the defence of the castle and the laws and liberties of the nation. I told him that he should be cautious in his attack, in case he shed yet more innocent blood.

A plan of the ground floor of Wardour Castle as it is today. Ludlow's rooms must have been on the side of the castle that is marked with a dotted line to show where the walls would have been before they were demolished. His room would have been on first floor, but the layout would have been similar on this side of the castle.

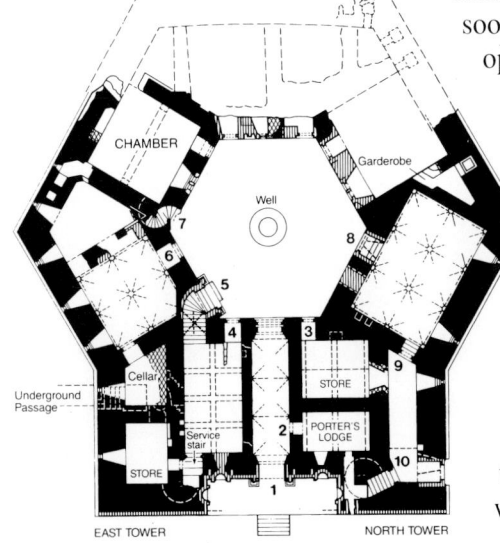

Two more nights passed. On the Thursday morning, being very weary, I lay down to sleep in my room. At some time between ten and eleven of the clock, one of our great guns fired at the enemy and dislodged a **match** they had left burning near some gunpowder in their mine. The mine exploded. I was flung up as it exploded, amid clouds of dust. As soon as the dust cleared I found both the doors of my room blown open, and my window towards the enemy blown open too, with so big a hole as you could have driven a cart through it. The party that had laid the mine had retired some distance, so as not to be hurt by the blast when it came. They now made haste to **storm** the castle – the rubble from my window had made them a path to it. The Irish yellow-coats, commanded by Captain Leicester, were the ones who came for me. My pistols were **wheel-locks**, and had been wound up all night; I could not get them to fire. I had to trust to my sword to keep back the enemy. I was, at first, alone in holding them off. There was no way into my room but through the courtyard window. I called through this window to the men that were there, telling them what had happened and requiring them to help at once.

Mr Gabriel Ludlow, my kinsman, came with others to my assistance and placed a ladder under the window. The ladder was some six feet short, so I had to leave the **breach**, where the enemy was ready to enter, several times to take his weapons and himself in. Then he helped in five or six more, who I ordered to fill up the breach and the doors with the bed, chairs, tables and all else to hand. My room being, to an extent, made safe, I went to see what other breaches had been made. I found one breach, in the room under me, which was well defended, but there was one in the gun room that was not defended at all. I put a guard there, and ran to the upper rooms, which had many doors and windows blown open, at every one of which I placed a guard in some way proportional to the danger. I then went up to the top of the castle, which was leaded, a six-angled shape, with a tower on each angle. Two of these were blown down, with part of the **leads**.

The enemy were sheltering behind the rubble. By throwing down some great stones, which their mine had plentifully provided, we killed one and wounded some others. Captain Leicester was one of those sheltering behind the rubble, and asked permission to carry off the wounded, which I allowed, saying we did not want to harm them, just to defend ourselves. Soon after, we had to make a request of their humanity. One of our soldiers, buried in the rubble outside, was yet alive, and sent word to me of his condition. So I sent to the enemy to ask them to dig him out and make him prisoner, or to allow us to rescue him. They refused to do either. When I said I had not used them in this way they said I did as I pleased, and, in the same way, their commander would do as he pleased. The poor man lived nearly three days longer before he died.

WHEEL-LOCK PISTOLS

During the Civil Wars there were three ways of lighting gunpowder to fire guns.

The **matchlock w**as simple but clumsy. Pulling the trigger put a lighted cord (called a match) into the firing pan where the gunpowder was. Almost all footsoldiers' muskets were matchlocks.

The **flintlock** was a new method, which used a flint to make a spark which lit the gunpowder. These guns were very expensive, so few troops had them.

The **wheel-lock** worked by winding up a spring so that when the trigger was pulled, the spring spun a wheel which made a spark. They were the favourite weapon of the cavalry. The danger was, if they were left wound up too long, as Ludlow's was, they might not fire.

Wardour Castle today, photographed from the side where the mine blew up the castle. The mine caused a great deal of damage, but not as much as the photograph suggests. After the Civil Wars, there was no attempt to repair the castle. When the Arundels returned to Wardour after 1660, they could not afford to repair it. They built a small house and some other buildings onto the non-ruined side, taking some of the stone from the ruined side to do so. The damaged walls were used as a sort of quarry for stone from then onwards, and it is hard to assess exactly how much of the damage was done by the original mine.

We lost three of our men in the blast from the mine, but the rest were safe. But our corn supplies which, eaten on the low ration we had set, would have fed us for a further three weeks, were blown up, as was much of our ammunition. We had some meat left, about enough for four days, so I thought it was best to hold out for as long as we could, hoping to get the best possible terms of surrender from the enemy. But Mr Balsum, our **minister**, with two or three other religious men, pressed me to make a treaty with the enemy at once. I told them that I did not wish to do this. We had beaten the enemy off, had three or four days' provisions, and would get better terms if we held on. They replied that if I did not listen to them, then any further blood that was spilt would be on my hands. This was a heavy charge to lay on me, and these were men whose wisdom, experience and faith I had a good opinion of, so I gave in to their request. The enemy commander refused to **parley**, saying we would not parley when the castle was whole, now he would not.

So now we had to prepare against the utmost extremity. No one had been shot during the storm, though some had been slightly wounded, and I had an enemy bullet pierce my hat close to my head. The besiegers had lost ten of their men, killed by shot. On Saturday we agreed a **truce** with the enemy; I had a conference with several of the enemy's officers at the breach in the castle walls. They urged me to surrender, and I said that I might, if we could agree terms, which would include us being free to go, with all our weapons and goods, to the nearest Parliamentary garrison. They said they were not sure that this could be agreed to, so I said that we would not surrender otherwise. They said the longer we held out the worse the terms would be, and that at least they were offering our lives, if not liberty. But I refused, so our treaty came to nothing.

I did wonder about charging out and through the enemy at night, heading for the nearest of our garrison, but we would have had to leave the sick and wounded. The spirits of my soldiers were very low. The enemy tried to lure several of my men to one end of the castle, the better to storm the other side, which, when I noticed, I tried to use the trickery of the enemy to animate our men afresh. Which it did, so much so that the enemy thought we had had news of relief coming from our side, and tried all night to talk our guards into surrendering us to the enemy in return for liberty. The next morning they came once more to the walls to treat for surrender.

The castle was now in such a poor state, as were we, that I said I would be willing to surrender, and be taken prisoner, if everyone else was free to go. They said they could not accept this. So I said I would surrender on four conditions. Firstly, no one was to be put to the sword. Secondly, none of my party was to be ill treated. Thirdly, none of us would be made prisoner at Oxford. Lastly, we would soon be exchanged for prisoners on their side. So they invited me to come out and discuss things further. Leaving my men on guard, I went to meet them. My Lord Arundel tried to persuade me to change sides. When I refused, he said he would do his best to get me quickly exchanged for his two sons, then prisoners with Sir William Waller. Sir Francis Doddington said they would agree to my terms, and wished that I would join them, but if I would not, then while I was his prisoner, my prison would be his own lodgings. So I returned to the castle and ordered my soldiers to lay down their arms. Then they were ordered into a secure room in the castle and placed under guard. I, my cousin Gabriel, Mr Balsum and a servant were not locked up, but had to promise not to escape.

This view of Wardour Castle is taken from the left side. On the walls to the left of the picture, you can see small circular marks that show where bullets went into the stone when the enemy fired muskets at the castle.

Chapter 4

A Prisoner!

The enemy did not keep their word as to the treatment of our men. They at once threatened the lives of two of them, men who had been forced to join the Royalists, but who ran away to join our cause. I went to see Captain Leicester to complain of this. He said he had made the treaty for our soldiers, and that these men were Royalist deserters, not my men. Had I wanted them included, he said, I should have named them at the time. I replied that I spoke of all in the castle, and that I would have died rather than surrender if I had known how they would be treated. He replied that he could always withdraw and leave us as they found us, which, as they now knew how bad a state we were in, was not a reasonable answer. I replied that his actions were so unfair that I did not doubt that God would give me a chance to put things right, or do so Himself. I was then sent for to go to the house where Sir Francis Doddington was staying. Here there was held some form of trial, which was no trial at all but a mockery of justice.

The two soldiers were condemned and executed, and the enemy talked of a trial for Mr Balsum too. They could find no evidence against him, so he was sent to Salisbury. But before this happened they tried to get rid of him by sending three men to kill him. They broke in on him while he was praying but they could not kill him. He looked so steadily at them that they confessed what they had been sent to do. They said they were so ashamed of what they had agreed to do that they would help him to escape, or do anything he said. He would not take the offer of escape, asking merely for a cloak to keep out the cold. Everyone else, including myself, were sent to prison in Oxford, which was also against the terms of our surrender. We were taken to Oxford by way of Salisbury and Winchester, and along the way there were several attempts made to get me to change sides, but I would not. When we arrived at Oxford I was sent, under guard, to a house near Christchurch until it was known what the King wanted done with me. I was then visited by the captain who had escorted me to Oxford, who said I was soon to be delivered to the keeper of the castle. He said that the keeper would take from me my upper garments, my money, and all else that was portable, and that I should give him these things, and he would smuggle them in to me in the morning. I, suspecting nothing, gave him my cloak, money and some other things, which he made off with. The keeper of the prison did not require any such thing and though I wrote to Sir Francis Doddington to complain, I got no reply. In the castle I found Mr Balsum, and many other friends who were in a similar situation.

I had a friend in Oxford who provided me with things that I needed. Those who had no friends were supplied with things from a fund collected for them in London. There were also people in Oxford who were a help, especially one minister, a Dr Hobbs.

PRISONS AND EXCHANGES

Prisoners of both sides were treated better at the beginning of the war than later. At first, there was a great deal of courtesy in dealing with prisoners, partly because the circumstances were new to both sides. As the war progressed and people lost members of their families, or heard rumours of mistreatment of prisoners by the other side, there was much less kindness. Sometimes prisoners were even hanged 'to teach the other side a lesson'.

Exchanges were made for prisoners on both sides. These prisoners were either captured in battle, or captured during sieges. Both sides tended to want to release fighting men rather than women and children. Both sides, too, were keen to try to get exchanges that benefited their side.

Oxford was a bad place to be a prisoner. Prisoners of the King had been badly treated generally, especially in Oxford, by Smith, the Marshall there. But there were men on the King's Council who had not lost their humanity. They examined Smith, found him unfit and replaced him with a man called Thorpe. While they were deciding this, Smith came to me under orders, saying that I could lodge where I pleased as long as I promised not to leave the town. But when I found I would not be allowed to visit my friends in prison I refused. The Lord Arundel tried to make good his promise of exchanging me for his two sons. He begged the King to do this. The King, however, refused, saying he had no use for children, and would exchange only for fighting men. Many people came to me in the hopes of my being exchanged for one of their relatives or friends. Among these were Lady Byron and friends of Sir Edward Stradling and Sir Hugh Pollard. Yet some of these exchanges seemed unequal to me; I did not want the enemy to benefit from any exchange made. The Earl of Essex was keen to make a quick exchange for me. In the end it was agreed that I would be exchanged, along with Colonel Houghton, Captain Sir John Saville and Captain Abercrombie, for Sir Edward Stradling, Colonel Lunsford and Sir Hugh Pollard.

I was led blindfold through the city of Oxford till I had passed their fortifications. Then I set out for London. I arrived there the next day, and arranged with the Earl of Essex an exchange for my officers and soldiers, which was soon made. He then made an exchange for Mr Balsum, who he then kept as his chaplain.

The City of Oxford, drawn by Wencleslas Hollar at about the time of Ludlow's imprisonment there. Oxford was the headquarters of the Royalists all through the Civil Wars. The castle and the prison can be seen to the right of the picture.

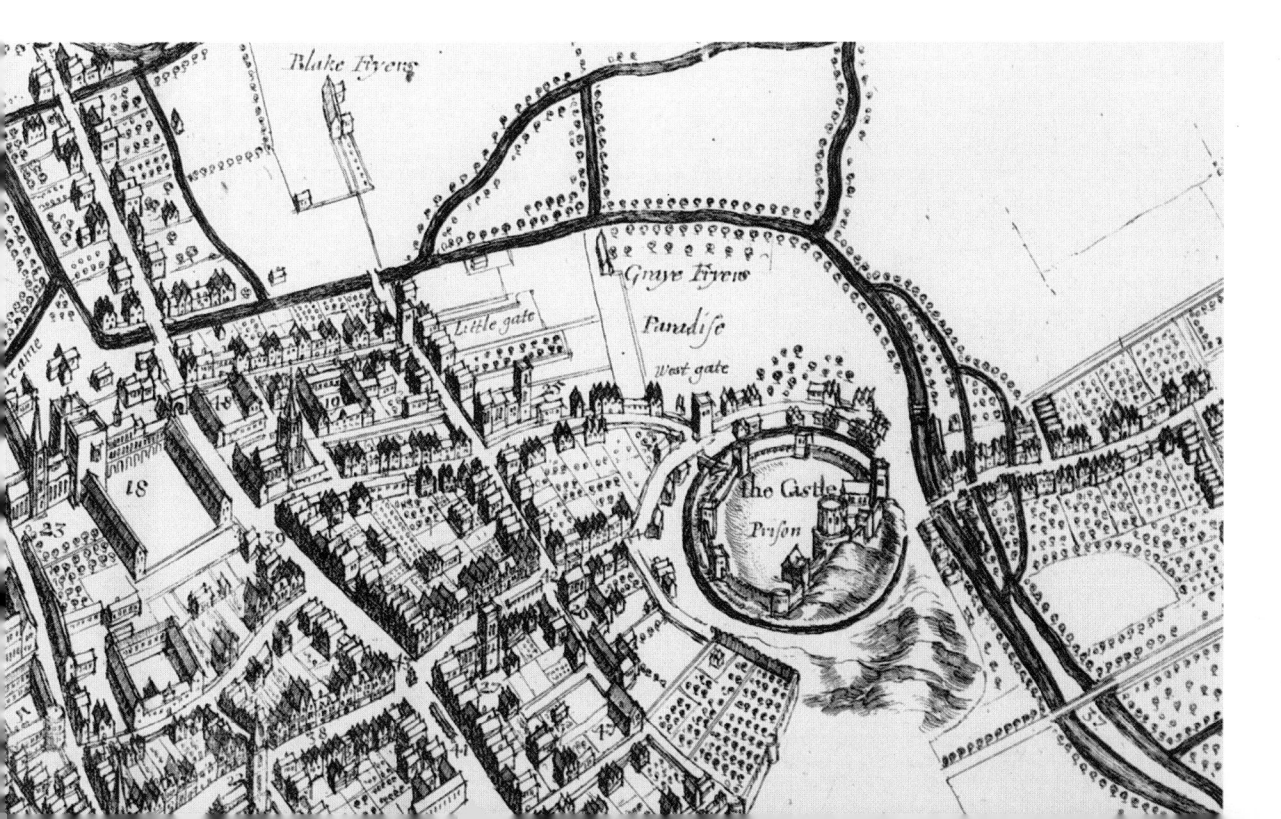

Chapter 5

Fighting in 1644

The Earl of Essex offered me a command in his army, but Parliament had appointed me Sheriff for Wiltshire, so I had to be in the west. Sir Arthur Hazilrigg offered me a place in his horse regiment under Sir William Waller. This was in the west, so I accepted taking the best of my old horse soldiers with me. As soon as my troop was ready, we joined Waller at Abingdon. He was told to block the King in Oxford from one side, while Essex did the same on the other. But the King left Oxford, and began to march towards Worcestershire. So the Earl of Essex commanded Sir William to pursue the King, while he, the Earl, went into the west. It was hard to see why this was decided this way, for most of us had joined Sir William on the understanding that we should remain in the west. We followed the King, but could not find a chance to engage him. Summer was nearly over, so several of us were sent back to the west, to raise more troops. I went back to Wiltshire.

Here we were told to go to relieve Major Wansley, who was besieged by the enemy in Woodhouse. We had a skirmish with a party of the enemy's horse on Warminster Heath, and heard from some prisoners we took that Sir Ralph Hopton, with 1,000 horse, was on his way to help the Royalists. The next morning we came on a party of the enemy's horse on the heath, hoping to lure us into chasing them, so that they could fall on our rear with some of their number hidden in the hedges. But we suspected their plan and marched off to Salisbury. When we reached the downs we saw the enemy. I observed them, and told Colonel Alexander Popham that they were at least four times our number. I advised him not to engage them, but he said that he was honour bound to do so. So he drew his party into one body of about a hundred, and I drew my troop into another body of a similar size. I was forced to go in search of my armour, telling my men to stand their ground until my return. As I was going back, I met Colonel Popham and all his party fleeing. When I asked what had caused him to change his mind, he said it was not advisable to fight them after all.

An illustration from a book of military instructions written at the time by Captain Nathaniel Burt. This gives instructions to dragoons on how to fire from horseback with a musket.

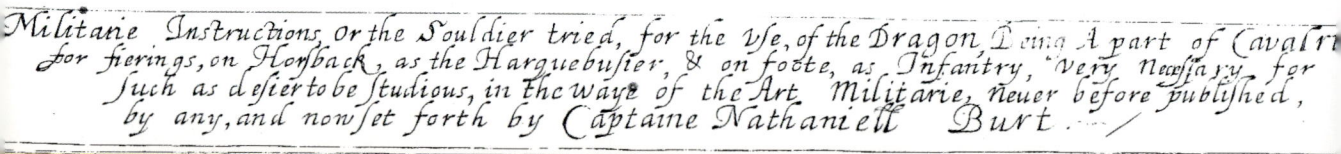

I found my men standing their ground, with the enemy advancing towards them in twelve bodies, each of which seemed as large as our one. We could not fight them, but I resolved to retreat in good order. I sent my standard in front, with some ten men, then rallied the rest to ride. But, seeing that some turned to flee, I put myself at the head of the troop and, in this way, managed to keep them together. After about three miles, one of my men fell from his horse, which ran off. The enemy were still pursuing us, so I took him up behind me. Luckily his horse soon rejoined the company, and was caught, and he could mount again. This was just as well, for my horse could no longer gallop with two on it. Two or three times the enemy sent men to catch up up with us, to demand surrender. We chased them off. Now many of the horses were tiring. I ordered the men to get off and kill these horses, so the enemy could not take them. The men themselves I ordered to take to the fields and hide in the corn or in nearby villages. Most of them did this, and were safe. A few were captured and killed in cold blood by the enemy.

I finally reached Salisbury with about thirty horse, where we were jeered at as we passed through. At this point we reached a place called Mutton Bridge, which I decided to hold against the enemy with some of my best fighters. I sent the rest of the troop on to Southampton while we held the bridge for some long time. The enemy had now chased us some twenty miles from where we first met with them. After our stand at the bridge they took no more of our men and we arrived safe at Southampton. Two days after our arrival Colonel Norton, who was besieging Winchester, was sent for to the siege at Basing House. He asked me to take his place in Winchester until his return. This I did, although my men were much in need of rest. So we marched there, and drew up in front of the castle. A troop of Royalist horse came out to meet us, one of whom was an old school fellow of mine. I was shot at by a musket loaded with two bullets – the first hit my horse, the second hit me, just on my breast plate. The horse carried me off, but died in the night.

My men were in need of rest, sleep, pay and many other things. I decided to return to Wiltshire, and sent a message to Colonel Norton to tell him of this. Then we marched back, by way of Salisbury, where I decided to provide for us from people known to favour the Royalist cause, probably the same as had jeered us several days before. I told them they had to raise, between them, £500 to pay and supply my men. They made excuses, and eventually I took £200 which I used to pay my men and supply them. When I had done this, I went to London to complete my regiment and get everything that it would need to function.

THE CAMPAIGN OF 1644

During 1643 the Royalist armies had had more success than those of Parliament. However, during the winter of 1643–4 Parliament made a deal with the Scots, who entered the war against the king. This meant that, in 1644, Parliament had five armies: the Scots, the Eastern Association, the Northern Army, and the armies in the south commanded by Essex and Waller. The plan was that the Scots, and the Northern and Eastern armies to capture the north, while Essex and Waller defeated the King's main army, which was based at Oxford.

The Royalists were beaten in the north, at Marston Moor. Waller and Essex, however, failed. They split their armies, and let Charles I escape from Oxford. Charles followed Waller's army and beat it at Cropredy Bridge. He then chased Essex's army into Cornwall, where he trapped it at Lostwithiel. Essex escaped by sea, and his cavalry escaped by land, but his footsoldiers had to surrender. What was left of Essex's and Waller's armies, and the army of the Eastern Association, fought the Second Battle of Newbury to try to stop Charles returning from the west. They lost. Parliament had not got any advantage from outnumbering Charles' forces.

> **SURGERY**
>
> Surgery in the Civil Wars was very rough and ready. Most troops tried to keep a surgeon with them, but in many cases they did more harm than good.
>
> As no one at the time knew about germs, there was no way to connect them to infection. Surgeons woked in conditions that were very unhygienic. By the time they had tried to dig a musket ball out of a man's wound with a probe that they had just used on another wounded man, the second wounded man was more likely to get an infected wound than if he had been left alone.
>
> Wounds got infected more often than not, and quickly became so badly infected that the only hope of saving a person was to cut off the affected part. Problems with this were that it could only be done if the wound was on an arm or leg. Also, major surgery without anaesthetics or antibiotics meant the patient was almost bound to die of shock or infection developed after the operation. Gabriel Ludlow would probabiy not have survived surgery, even if the surgeon had been prepared to treat him.

We got word that the enemy had garrisoned both Sturton House and Sir Ralph Hopton's house at Witham. We marched first to Sturton House, which they tried to hold against us. We set fire to one of the gates, and the fire spread to a nearby room and through the castle. The garrison slipped away under cover of darkness. Having made sure the castle could no longer be fortified, we went to Witham. Here we found nearly 100 cattle in the park, which served as further payment for my soldiers. The garrison did not fight, but asked to retreat, which we allowed as long as they gave up their arms. While we were engaged in this way, the main body of our army was meeting with that of the King and there was news brought to us of a great battle on Marston Moor, which both sides gave out that they had won, yet ours was the victory.

The Second Battle of Newbury

As the war moved to the west I was called to join Sir William Waller and his party near Basingstoke. We went there with some 500 horse, and were very well received. We then advanced on Newbury, which the enemy had taken. We could not approach from the south, because the town was guarded by a river. To the north-west was Donnington Castle. Only the north-east had a sort of access to the town. The ground between the road and the river was marshy and impassable – the road was the only access, and this was guarded by an earthwork and numbers of footsoldiers in the houses on the outskirts of the town.

Little was done the first day, except for a few small skirmishes. On our side we had the advantage of the hill, which provided our men with some sort of cover. Here too, we were able to put our field pieces, with a good line of fire on the town. The townspeople then moved their guns to fire on the exposed side of the hill, which my regiment were guarding that day. The firing of the guns caused a lot of damage. One of the wounded was my cousin, Gabriel Ludlow, who was with me in the siege of Wardour. He did not die immediately after he was shot. I got him out of the way of their guns, then called a surgeon. His stomach and bowels were torn open, and his hip-bone was shattered. He regained his senses, but the surgeon refused to treat him, saying he was bound to die anyway. The manner of his death troubled me much.

We were forced to divide our army. One half was sent to attack on the north-west side of the town, near to the castle, which we did with such vigour that they were forced to quit their ground, and run to the castle for shelter, leaving behind several cannon and many men killed. The Earl of Manchester's men, on the other side, seeing the enemy routed there, made up their minds to do as well. Our horse and foot were drawn up near the road and attacked the houses so fiercely that, despite the enemy firing hard at us, they were forced to pull back to their earthwork.

Our horse stood near the earthworks while the foot attacked, to keep off any enemy horse. Several of my men and horses were shot during the engagement. Night separated us. Under cover of darkness, the enemy moved all their weapons into Donnington Castle itself, then, just before day came, they marched off between our two groups, to join the King at Oxford.

Next morning our armies joined to follow the enemy. It was the biggest body that I saw all through the war, some 7,000 horse and dragoons. But we could not catch up with them, they had too good a start. Why we did not sieze the arms in Donnington Castle and then march on the King at Oxford, I do not know. There were many who did not want such a general engagement. The army leaders and those of Parliament argued over this. I went with Waller to the siege of Basing House but things broke up and I returned home to Wiltshire. Both sides set about fortifying towns for the winter.

The siege of Aire-sur-la-Lys by Peeter Snayers, painted in 1641. Aire-sur-la-Lys is in northern France, and its defences were bigger and more complex than any that would have been found in England at the time. The theory of fortification in the 1640s was to build low walls, usually filled with earth. This meant the walls were harder to hit with canon fire (because they were low), and less likely to fall down (because the earth-filled wall absorbed the impact of the canon ball). The walls were built in straight sections with sharp angles, so that canon from one wall could fire along the next section of wall at any attackers approaching it. English soldiers, also without uniforms, would have looked like those shown here.

After my return to Wiltshire I was told to send what men I could spare to reinforce a party commanded by Major General Holborn, who was ordered to march into the west to relieve Colonel Blake, besieged by the enemy in Taunton. I gathered 200 horse for this, and had to lead them myself, for my major had got possession of good quarters in Deane, and was not willing to move. We were joined on our march by other troops, including some from Dorset. When we were advanced near the enemy, my troop was ordered to a part that was occupied by the enemy, but their men left when they saw us approaching. The enemy abandoned the siege soon after our arrival, a thing that we had not expected at all. So we provisioned the town and all went home.

On my return to Salisbury, I was told the enemy had garrisoned Langford House, just two miles away. I decided to be ready for an attack. I set my workmen to fortifying parts of the town. That night I drew up my regiment to explain the need to be watchful and to appoint a guard for the night, when word came that the enemy was coming, and had reached Amesbury. I sent sixty men with Captain Sadler (the only officer I had left, some being absent with permission, others being absent without it) towards the enemy. They had orders to find out as much as they could about the enemy and their intentions. We set out to follow the advance troop, and were sent news, first of sighting of the enemy, and then that Captain Sadler had engaged with the enemy and could not now get away.

So we hastened to his aid, and found the enemy outnumbered all of my troop. But there was nothing to do but go to Sadler's aid, which I did, giving the order to charge when we were nearer. But they, before we came within a pistol shot, ran away. So I divided my men into two groups, taking command of one group myself and giving command of the other not to Sadler, whose troops were very dissatisfied with his conduct, but to a man called Marshall. We gave chase to the enemy, and killed some and captured others.

The buff coat and helmet of a New Model Army soldier. The buff coat is made of thick leather. It was thick enough to stand quite a severe blow from a sword, while being more flexible than armour. Sometimes armour was worn over the back and chest, leaving the arms free. The helmet is called a 'lobster pot' because the pieces at the back that protect the neck look like a lobster's shell. The bars on the front of the helmet do not obscure the soldier's view, but protect the face from most sword slashes.

On our return to the town I had the prisoners shut up, under guard, and put men on guard till morning came. Word came that the enemy was in the town. So I and six others mounted up, and ordered the rest to follow. As we rode we heard a great noise in the street that leads to the city from Old Sarum, so we returned to the market place, to find it, too, swarming with enemy horse. So we went by the backstreets to where we had left the guard, to find that there were far fewer there than we expected, for some, against orders, had gone to bed, and others had run away, so there were only about thirty horse remaining. Of these I ordered ten to charge, while I followed on with the rest. A trumpeteer followed us, sounding his trumpet as if there were more to come. The town was full of the enemy. We had a troop of men fortifying the belfrey. Most of my men had scattered, so I hid our standard at a supporter's house and, delivering my prisoners to the belfrey, I and about six others retreated by way of the Close, where I lodged with a Mrs Sadler. A boy was at the door with my armour, which I put on. I gathered some twenty men, and went to the belfrey, where our men advised us to meet the enemy, which we went to do, and met them at the North Gate, almost their whole body. I ordered the guard to fire on them and I and as many of my men as would go charged them, firing as we went. They began to give ground, then daylight came, and showed them the smallness of our number, so I was forced to retire as fast as I could with my men, one of whom carried away an enemy sword through his arm. We drew up near the top of Harnham Hill, and fired at the enemy but then had to retreat. I then gathered as many of my men as I could find and marched to Southampton. Here I tried to get aid to relieve our men in the belfrey at Salisbury. But news came that the enemy had burned down the door and our men had had to surrender. The enemy took some eighty prisoners, and would have taken more, had not some of their guards quitted their posts, so many of our men escaped. I was wounded on the chest with a sword, my horse was shot, and died soon after. I went back to London to raise supplies for my regiment.

In September, Parliament decided to send a gift to Lord Fairfax for his services and I volunteered to be part of the guard, for this was an opportunity to go back into the west, which was not easily done, for there were many of the King's army hovering on the downs, so I took a guard of some twenty or thirty men with me and then joined Colonel Massey's party, commanded by Edward Cook. We got news of a Royalist party going to relieve those we were besieging at Corfe Castle. Before we could get any men together they surprised some of our men near Warham, took supplies into the castle and headed back for Oxford. And so the war dragged on, until, in February 1646, it was time to elect a new Parliament.

THE NEW MODEL ARMY

Ludlow does not mention the New Model Army, but it was one of the most important reasons why Parliament won the war. In the winter of 1644, after the defeats that Ludlow described, the MPs decided to set up a proper army. This army was to have uniforms, to be properly trained and to be paid regularly.

The army was to consist of 22,000 men. There were fewer to begin with. It was to have eleven cavalry regiment of 600 men each and a single regiment of 1,000 dragoons (who rode to battle but most often dismounted to fight). They were to be paid two shillings [10p] a day. These men were soon found. But it was hard to find enough footsoldiers. There were supposed to be 12,000 men, organized into companies of equal sizes. They were only to be paid eight pence [3p] a day, about the same wage as an ordinary farm worker, for a much more dangerous job.

But enough men were found, and trained, to give Parliament a real army of fighting men, rather than a collection of people who wanted to fight. When the fighting began again in 1645 the New Model Army won one of the most decisive victories of the war at the Battle of Naseby. They went on winning.

Chapter 6

Parliament and the Army

PARLIAMENT DIVIDED

The supporters of Parliament in the Civil War knew they didn't want the country ruled as Charles I had ruled it, but they could not agree on what they did want.

There were two main groups in Parliament. The **Presbyterians** wanted to compromise with the King, and set up a national Presbyterian church which everyone would have to belong to. The **Independents** were determined there should be no national church. They wanted everybody to be free to join the church of their choice.

There were also important groups that were not in Parliament. The most important of these was the **New Model Army**. Many Army officers were Independents. Some of the soldiers were **Levellers** – they wanted ordinary men to be able to vote, as well as the rich and middle classes. (Nobody thought women should vote.)

We were concerned that the Parliament would not have men elected to it who would then give the King by treaty what he had not been able to take in war. My father, who had been an MP for Wiltshire, had died and Sir James Thynne, the other MP, had deserted to the King. I got a letter from the Earl of Pembroke, asking me to stand as an MP, along with his son. This young man, the Earl said, though young, was an honest man. I replied that if the county chose to elect me I would do my best to serve it honestly. I had several letters asking me to attend the election, so I went, and was elected without opposition. When I reached the House of Commons I met with Colonel Robert Blake, who had been chosen for Taunton, and we went in together to swear the usual oaths and sit.

Much of our business was taken up with the war, and raising men and money. At this time we also captured Sir Jacob Astley, a close friend of the King, who said the Royalists were well aware of the divisions in our party, which had begun the war united by a single cause. Indeed, they were working to deepen the rifts between various groups and to get men on their side. We certainly found that many of the Parliament were neutral in the matter of the war, or in favour of a quick treaty. The Scots and the City of London sided with this group, who I felt were against the **commonwealth**.

Meanwhile the Scots demanded some £200,000 in pay for their work for Parliament, and advised a peace with the King. Parliament asked for an exact account of the Scots' expenses, and asked them to withdraw from the country, so there was a falling out. The terms offered by the King were rejected, and a siege of Oxford was ordered, but the King slipped away before the siege could be set. We found the King had gone to the Scots at Newcastle – this had been arranged in secret before. The Scots having the King in their power pressed him to act as they wished, and pressed Parliament to send peace proposals to the King. At this time some brigades were disbanded, partly because of the cost of keeping them and also the earnest desire of many of them to return home.

The House was now divided on many matters. One group were set on peace, a disbandment of the army, and a repression of those groups such as Independents whom they saw as firebrands. Another group, consisting of Independents and the like, encouraged **Army** officers to demand their arrears of pay in a manner that offended Parliament. So Parliament decided to send the Army out of the way to Ireland, which many in the Army refused to do. Five regiments of horse chose leaders called Agitators, who drew up a petition to Parliament refusing to disband until the Army had been paid and the running of the kingdom was settled.

Parliament was angry and there was a move to have the petitioners sent to the Tower. At last Parliament simply declared that the Army should not meddle with the governing of the country, or present petitions that were not approved by their General. So they got up another petition, and this time it was presented through their General. There were now even more in the House who thought the petitioners were traitors. They said that the Army was the servant of Parliament and that its members should obey, not make demands. The debate about whether to imprison the petitioners went long into the night, when at last Mr Denzil Hollis proposed that they should declare the petition seditious, but only after a certain day. There would be a pardon for all those who withdrew from the petition before that time. Some of us feared the consequences of even this less extreme action. We made the mistake of leaving the House, which allowed for more severe votes against the way the Army was behaving to be passed.

The Agitators now saw that they would soon be at the mercy of Parliament, unless they acted. They had to give in or do something to get the upper hand. On 4 June, 1647, they sent a party of horse, commanded by Cornet Joyce to Holmby House to sieze the King.

Copies of some of the standards of the Parliamentarian army. They can show us some of the things that the soldiers felt were important about the war. These were the things that they would want put right after the war was won. Having fought hard, they would not be happy to accept many compromises with what they wanted. Unfortunately, not everyone who fought for Parliament against the King wanted the same things.

Chapter 7

The Second Civil War

Now I must tell you how it was that the King was not with the Scots. In August, peace proposals were again sent to him. The Scots pressed him to accept, but he refused. The Scots gave him to Parliament. He was taken to Holmby House, from where the Army faction took him. The Independents treated the King with such care he warmed to them, being sure that once any party put him back on the throne he would enjoy all his old power and keep no promises made under threat.

The Army now drew up an act of treason against eleven MPs, for betraying the Parliamentary cause by trying to break up the Army. They did this not because they wanted to execute the MPs but because they thought, rightly, that the MPs would withdraw from Parliament and cause the Army no more trouble. The Army had now managed to make enemies of the Parliament, the Scots and the City of London, so they had to be kinder to the King, which was explained to me by Ireton as merely a way of keeping all quiet. Now Royalists who had fled to France began to return and negotiations between the King and the Army seemed to go well. Yet the King did not fully trust the Army, nor they him, so when Parliament voted that the King should be moved to Richmond it looked as though he might accept. Finally he himself insisted on a move to Windsor. The Army saw he was turning from them, and pressed him for an agreement to proposals they had made to him. The King, finding himself courted on all sides by the Army, Independents, Presbyterians and many others, felt he could do as he pleased, and kept all in the air. This could not go on forever. The King rejected the Army's proposals in July, 1647. He now encouraged Parliament with the promise of peace proposals. Parliament argued about negotiaitions with the King. Several of us, including myself, decided to leave and join the Army for our own protection. The next day we met with the Army on Houndslow Heath.

A print from the time showing Charles I in prison in Carisbrooke Castle. Charles fled from army 'custody' in Hampton Court to the Isle of Wight because he could see that the Army were getting impatient with his refusal to settle anything. On 11 November, in the afternoon, he slipped away and rowed across the river, where two friends were waiting with horses.

He hoped that he would find support on the Isle of Wight. The Governor of the Ise of Wight was Colonel Hammond, a Parliamentarian, who was said to be against the Army. The Royalists hoped to get him to change sides. Hammond would not change sides, but he gave Charles enough freedom to be able to negotiate with the Scots (something Hammond had not intended to happen). On Boxing Day, 1647, Charles signed an agreement with the Scots. When Hammond discovered this he changed the conditions of Charles' imprisonment, and when Charles tried to leave, he found he could not. Many plots were formed to help Charles escape – he would try to plot with anyone he came into contact with – guards, washerwomen, servants, visitors. None of them succeeded.

We were brought news that the Commons had waited some time for the Speaker, who was one of our number, and when he did not arrive elected another, and were trying to raise men in London to fight the Army. They also set up negotiations with the King, which he was, as ever, slow in considering. Things became confused; rumours of both settlement and fighting between the Army and Parliament spread. At last we could resume our seats in the House. As we came in so others left. All was confused, and matters between all sides and the King were uncertain. There were still treaties being offered to the King. He still saw all and agreed to nothing. He was also in secret negotiations with the Scots, still looking for an agreement to his best advantage. He decided to escape to the Isle of Wight. He and some friends went there, against the advice of some who said the governor might not support him. The Army sent letters to the governor of Carisbrooke Castle, telling him to keep the King under guard. This he did.

From his prison on the Isle of Wight the King continued to negotiate with all sides. It became clear that he could not be trusted and would agree to nothing with the Army or Parliament; that he was hopeful of getting the Scots to invade on his behalf and so, on 3 January, 1648, Parliament voted not to negotiate with him again. At the same time the Scots raised an army for the King and the country divided yet again. Various towns and castles declared support for the King, and fighting began again. I went down to Wiltshire once again to raise two regiments of foot and one of horse. At first things looked black, for many who had been for Parliament in the first war seemed now to incline to the King. But our army fought hard. When the Scots were beaten at the Battle of Preston, in August 1648, we had all but won.

Parliament began negotiations with the King in September. The Army told Parliament that they should not treat with the King, after all that went before. Parliament pressed the King for a quick answer, to settle before the Army could act. But the King, as ever, was indecisive. The Army came to London and met with those of us who were concerned about negotiations with the King. It was decided that the Army would stand guard on the House of Commons the next day, allowing in only those who had been true to the country's interest. They justified this 'purge', carried out by a Colonel Pride, by saying the members were kept out for trying to raise men against the Army in July. The King was brought to Windsor; there was much debate as to what should be done with him. The Army wanted to bring the King to trial at once, for warring on Parliament and the people of England. Others wanted first to decide how the country should be run without a King, for they feared the Army would take over the government of the country. It was finally resolved that there could be no trial without a law to allow it.

THE SECOND CIVIL WAR AND AFTER

The Second Civil War broke out in 1648 and was the result of the scheming of Charles I after the First Civil War had ended. Charles, while negotiating with all groups, had reached an agreement with the Scots. They invaded to help him. But they were quickly beaten by the New Model Army at Preston.

PRIDE'S PURGE

There were still enough Presbyterian MPs in the House of Commons to win a vote for a compromise with Charles. This did not suit the Independents or their allies in the Army, where the officers and men were agreed that Charles must pay the price for starting the Second Civil War. The Army was the main source of power, so its view was decisive. Colonel Pride, with a number of soldiers, stood at the door of Parliament. He stopped those MPs who supported the Presbyterians from going in. They would not be there to vote.

Chapter 8

Trial and Execution of the King

The House of Commons voted, on 1 January, 1649, that 'by the fundamental laws of the land, it is treason for the King of England, for the time being, to war against the Parliament and kingdom.' The Lords would not agree to this law being passed, so the House of Commons passed the law without the consent of the Lords, saying that they, the elected people of the country, were the supreme power of the nation, for they represented the people. Then several petitions were brought to Parliament from all over the country, asking that the King be brought to justice. So they passed an Act authorizing thirty people to hold the trial and the condemnation, or acquittal, of the King. They also empowered these people, if the King was condemned, to pass sentence and see that sentence was carried out. The High Court of Justice met on 8 January, 1649. It consisted of about eighty MPs, army officers and gentlemen of the country. They chose various officers with Sergeant Richard Bradshaw as their President. A charge of high treason was drawn up against the King and a place was prepared in Westminster Hall for his public trial. It was decided that the King should have a guard of thirty men during the trial, and Bradshaw a guard of twenty men.

All things now being ready for the trial, the King was then moved from Westminster to St James'. From there the King was taken, on 2 January, 1649, to the bar of the High Court of Justice, where he was told of the reason for his being there.

Richard Bradshaw was not the first person to be asked to be the judge at Charles I's trial, but he was the first one to accept. He was, however, as aware as the others who had been asked of the dangers that went with the job. He had a guard, as Ludlow points out, to keep possible assassins away. He also took other precautions. This is the hat he wore during the trial of the King. It was an ordinary seventeenth century hat, reinforced with bands of iron.

The charge was that, contrary to the trust put in him by the people to see laws made for their good, he had used his power to subvert those laws, and govern for his own advantage. This had led him to suppress and then war with Parliament, which had caused many deaths, for which he was on trial. The King interrupted the reading of the charges against him, saying that he was not entrusted with power by the people, that the people were his by inheritance, and demanding to know what authority they had to try him. When they answered that an Act made by the Commons, who were elected by the people, he replied that Parliament could not act in this way to their king. He was told that Parliament could acknowledge no king but God, and demanded that the King answer the charge, guilty or not guilty. The King refused to plead, saying that no man could call him to account, certainly not the court as it stood; he was accountable only to God for his actions. He then talked long of not understanding how the Parliament could have called him here to try him, when he had been engaged in negotiations with the commissioners while on the Isle of Wight. President Bradshaw said that this was not a relevant discussion, that the King should answer the charge. He would not. The Court said that if he would give no answer they would proceed as if he had pleaded guilty.

Then the King was taken from the courtroom, and the Court met to decide what was now to be done. They decided that to be sure that people thought the trial was fair they would call the King again to answer the charges twice more, in public, before giving judgement. Twice more the King was called, on 22 January and 23 January, and twice he answered as he had the first time. All these three occasions were duly witnessed. Now the Court deliberated on the charge against the King. They announced that the King was a tyrant, traitor, murderer and a public enemy to the commonwealth. They said that because of this he should be executed. It was also decided that the President should not permit the King to speak after sentence was pronounced. He should openly declare that the King had had his chance to speak before, but that he had refused to accept the authority of the court.

In the afternoon the King was brought to the bar and asked permission to make a proposal that he thought would satisfy eveyone, before sentence was passed. This was a suggestion that he should resign his place, and that his son should rule instead. They retired, and considered the matter, but ruled that they had no authority to do anything but try him for the crime as set out. They could not accept proposals, which should have been made to Parliament before, there having been plenty of time to do so.

> **WHY EXECUTE THE KING?**
> There were many debates over what to do with the King once he was beaten. This were not helped by the fact that he not behaved in a trustworthy manner during the prolonged peace negotiations. So, if he was kept alive he could not be trusted, and would prove a rallying point for Royalists no matter if he was imprisoned in England or anywhere else.

The Court then called the King for sentence, and ran over his crimes and the chances he had had to answer to them. The President enlarged on the horrid nature of the King's crimes, the crimes of which he stood convicted. He said the only just power of kings surely came from the people; yet the King had tried, through the whole of his reign, to subvert the good laws that had been made at the will of the people who had given him his power. He had tried to introduce an **arbitrary** and tyrannical government, in which the people had no say at all, trying either to corrupt Parliaments to agree with him, or to suppress them altogether. Yet worse was to come for, when he had agreed that he would not dissolve Parliament, yet he had raised an army against it, to dissolve it forever. This war, which he had begun, had cost countless people in England their lives. So now, as God commanded, and the nation expected, he was brought to answer for these crimes and the court found him guilty of them. The sentence was read to the King, that he should, for the crimes he had been charged with, be taken from the court to the place he came from, and be taken from there to a place of execution, where his head would be severed from his body. The King would now have spoken, but the law now forbade this after the passing of sentence, as had been agreed by the court before they met with him to pass sentence.

The High Court of Justice now decided that Whitehall would be a suitable place for the execution. A scaffold was ordered to be erected near the Banqueting House and covered with black. On 29 January, 1649, a warrant was signed for the execution of the King. Some sixty people signed the warrant, of which I was one. He was allowed Dr Juxton, once Bishop of London, to attend him and read a sermon to him and administer the **sacrament**. The Duke of Gloucester and the Lady Elizabeth were allowed time to say farewell to him.

The next day, at about eight in the morning, the King, attended by a guard, was brought from St James' Palace to Whitehall, where he was faced with a wait of some two hours. He was allowed to drink a glass or two of wine and then was taken to the scaffold out of a window in the Banqueting House. He made a speech, took off his St George's Cross, and knelt down at the block. The executioner then did his duty. It was ordered that the body should be buried at Windsor. The burial was carried out without further delay. The Duke of Lennox, the Marquis of Hereford, the Earls of Southampton and Lindsey, with some others, attended the burial, having been given permission by Parliament to do so. Others who had been on the King's side were less considerate of his memory – they made the best speed they could to flee, fearing that if the King were executed, then they might also lose their lives, if they were to be caught by their enemies. Some were, indeed, caught and locked in the Tower of London.

Now an Act was passed that the House of Lords was useless, and was to be abolished, and also that 'a King in this nation is unnecessary, burdensome and dangerous to the liberty, safety and public interest of the people,' that monarchy should be abolished and the nation should be governed as a commonwealth. They ordered all seals that had the image of the King on them to be destroyed, and had a new one made, with the House of Commons on one side and on the other a cross and a harp, the arms of England and Ireland, and the inscription 'God is with us'. There were then some executions and some reprieves of those who had commanded in the King's army in both wars. Parliament then decided to set up a Council of State, appointed by five of their members, of which I was one. We chose some thirty-five persons, four Lords, the rest commoners. These people examined the MPs in the Commons before they sat, to make sure that they had no Royalist sympathies.

The execution of Charles I, painted at the time. Not everyone was in favour of the execution. There were those who saw it was necessary, but many people who had fought for Parliament opposed it. Lord Fairfax, a leading figure in the Army, refused to attend the trial, or be involved at all. His wife went to the trial, and had to be thrown out for calling out that it was illegal. The scaffold was surrounded by soldiers to control the crowd. Reports from the time speak of 'a great groan' going up from the crowd as the axe fell. We must be careful about believing accounts from the time – most people had strong feelings about the execution, and would give a biased account of the way the crowd reacted.

Chapter 9

England Without a King

Ludlow in Ireland

We faced opposition to our government both in Ireland and Scotland and it was necessary for our army to fight in both places. We raised money for these wars by various means, such as selling off land that had belonged to the church, the King or Royalists. But we also had to tax the country, which, for the most part paid gladly, knowing it was for the country's good and that we ourselves were paying as much in tax as they did. A Committee was set up to decide how to run the elections to be held as soon as the nation was safe from enemies abroad and at home. This was in January 1650, at about the same time as Lieutenant General Cromwell returned from fighting to take his seat in the Parliament again. He was returned from Ireland, was made Captain-General of all the land forces and set out in June against the Scots.

I was now appointed, being an MP and one of the Council of State, to go to Ireland as Lieutenant General of the Horse. I asked not to do this, yet was overruled, and had to go. So I went to serve under the Lord Deputy Ireton, and found the country in a deperate plight, being visited by both famine and sickness to an extreme degree. We fought hard both in battles and sieges; we seemed to do well, yet we were never entirely the victors. I was sent from place to place, with orders to subdue resistance with a severity which I found hard to use. I was sent, in November 1651, to Clare Castle, which we were besieging. I was in a very low state. I camped for the night on a hill near the castle, and caught, by reason of the severe weather, a very dangerous cold. The next day the enemy left the castle. I was far worse, but did not like to leave my men, so wrapped myself in my buff coat, then a fur coat, then an oiled one. Yet when we quartered for the night I was so sick that my men had to ride on without me, and I stayed with a guard, yet got no better, so rode on in the filthy weather to catch up with my men. In this foul weather the poor footsoldiers were obliged to wade through an estuary, often up to their waists in water. Yet we reached Carrickgaholt Castle and induced them to surrender too. Then we met with the Lord Deputy, who also fell sick and, neglecting his health, died. Parliament sent to me, to make me Lord Deputy, yet I did not feel equal to the task, and begged them to send someone else to do the job. But they would not heed me. While there were many Irish coming to lay down their arms, yet others held out, in places like Connaught and Ulster. Now there was a move in Parliament to replace me and, though there were some who wanted me to stay, Cromwell wanted Fleetwood to take my place. So, while I spent the summer of 1652 much as I had spent the summer before, in June, Fleetwood was given a commission to take my place. I was glad when, in September, 1652, he arrived for all my care and troubles in this post had been rewarded by nothing but envy and hatred. Yet I had to stay as his deputy.

IRELAND

Ireland was a separate island with a separate language and culture and the Irish did not want to be part of Britain. Most of them were Catholic; this made relations with England even more strained once England became a Protestant country. In the 1550s the English started to send people in large numbers to settle in various parts of Ireland. This policy was called plantation – 'planting' English people in the hope that their ways would take root. It continued into the reign of Charles I. In October 1641 the Irish Catholics rebelled and killed many English Protestants.

The Commonwealth did not change policies in Ireland. They took over in Ireland and kept a permanent army there to keep control. They sold yet more Irish land to English Protestants, or gave it to soldiers instead of pay.

Fleetwood brought news that Parliament had granted several adventurers land in Ireland which had been taken from the rebels. They also used this land to pay off money owing to soldiers there. There was no new Parliament, but progress had been made in deciding how to divide up the country for elections. By March 1653 we were no longer at war. There was a general expectation of an election. And it was now that Cromwell, risen high in the Army and in Parliament, showed his hand. We in Ireland were too far from matters to affect them; we could only hear the news in horror.

[At this point Cromwell, fearing that Parliament would never hold elections, forced the Parliament to dissolve, bringing soldiers into the House of Commons to drive them all out. This horrified people like Ludlow because when Charles I had tried to do this (it was illegal) it had been a step towards civil war. Cromwell then set up elections where MPs were nominated rather than elected, to make sure they had the 'right' opinions. This Parliament, called the Barebones Parliament, dissolved itself, giving power back to Cromwell. A Council of Army officers met and drew up a document called *An Instrument of Government*. This gave Cromwell the power to run the country as 'Lord Protector', in a form of limited monarchy. (See box on page 41.)]

The Seal of the Commonwealth from 1651. It shows the House of Commons sitting with the Speaker in the big chair. There was no House of Lords at this time, nor any other 'single person' (as Ludlow puts it) in power. The Commons ran the country.

A portrait of Oliver Cromwell by Samuel Cooper. Cromwell was a Puritan; he believed deeply in God and doing his duty to God. He was an MP and sided with Parliament in the Civil War. In 1645 he helped to organize the New Model Army. He hoped the Commonwealth would work as a republic after the execution of the King. Problems between the Army and Parliament led to trouble. From 1649 until his death he tried to get them to agree. He replaced the Rump (see box on page 41) with another Parliament. This did not work either, so he bowed to pressure from the Army to lead the Government, taking the title 'Protector'. Ludlow said Cromwell wanted to be King. This is a biased view. Cromwell was offered the crown several times, but always refused it.

Changes in government

I resolved to oppose Oliver Cromwell's **usurpation**, or at least to do nothing to help it in Ireland. When the time came to proclaim him Protector here I refused to sign the acceptance, which, as a member of the Commission, I should have done. So a secretary signed 'in the name of the Commission', so it was not obvious that anyone had refused to sign. I decided to act no longer as a Commissioner, in case I seemed to accept Cromwell as a lawful authority. I was persuaded by Fleetwood to still go to meetings and advise, but I did not vote, or sign any order. Yet my military role, given to me by Parliament, I did not feel able to give up.

Cromwell now sent his son, Henry, to Ireland. I told him of my dissatisfaction with the state of England. I agreed to continue the military side of my work, but said I saw less need for the military to be kept on, now the wars were over. In May, 1654, elections were to be held, according to the rules of the Instrument of Government, which were, indeed, much more equal and just than the old ones. Many people of integrity and virtue were chosen. I was chosen for Wiltshire. When Parliament was to meet, Cromwell travelled there in a coach, with an army guard, and went to the Abbey, in kingly dress, to hear a sermon. Then he made a speech to the MPs, trying to show that things had fallen out as they did not by his **contrivance**, but by the hand of God. Then he excluded some MPs he did not want – this after there had been many underhand methods used in elections to exclude any he disliked. Now the MPs fell to debate over the Instrument. When he heard this, Cromwell put a guard on the door, and told them they could not query the Instrument – for it had led to them being called – so no one could sit in Parliament if they did not agree with it. Some MPs withdrew, not liking the force used in the matter, but most agreed. Now Cromwell, to establish his dynasty, set Fleetwood in second place to his son, Henry, in Ireland, and put many of his friends in places of power. Despite the fact that Parliament had agreed with him, he did not think them sufficiently inclined to serve his designs and wishes.

Cromwell accused Parliament of trying to bring about disorder by meddling with the Instrument, and failing to make provision for the Army. He dissolved Parliament – losing himself the affection of the people by this act. He now divided England into twelve regions, each run by a Major General of his choosing. Many people were unhappy with this. I was one of them, and this caused me to be relieved of my military duties in Ireland. I was told to give up my commission. I said I dared not do so to any but Parliament. I was then told that I must give my commission up or return to England a prisoner. I refused to give up my commission to any but Parliament. I was offered the choice of imprisonment in Ireland or England and chose London, but Fleetwood persuaded me to wait a while, saying that things in England were too confused at present, as they were.

For Cromwell was throwing lives away abroad (in the fighting in the West Indies) and liberties away at home (those who rebelled were not merely losing their lives, many were being deprived of their lands, and whole droves were being transported abroad). After four months, I prepared to go to England; an order was sent forbidding me to go. Then Fleetwood was called to England. He gave me a pass to go to England a month later. I was unsure what to do, but decided to set off at the time set down in the pass. We had a stormy crossing. We were met by the governor of Beaumaris Castle, who seemed melancholy, and the reason, we found, was because a Captain Shaw had arrived with an order for my arrest, despite my pass from Fleetwood. I was taken to a lodging where I was placed under guard. After six weeks Captain Shaw returned and I was taken to London, where I met with Oliver Cromwell, who was now being called 'his Highness' there. We spoke at length, and I also spoke to his Council, explaining my position. I was not imprisoned, but was not allowed to sit as an MP.

In 1656 the usurper now seemed to think the Instrument lay too great a restraint on him, and set about trying to establish for his family a crown and the succession, by making himself king. So a Parliament was called, with which, even though it offered him the crown, he could not get on, so it too was dissolved. The Army in England and Ireland were unhappy with Cromwell's kingly ambitions. Despite his attempts to keep all parties happy, there were many plots against his life from all sides, which he repressed with the utmost severity. He had, at this time, many infirmities, which made him very ill. I decided to go to London, which he was told of, and which made him suspect that I might try to set a rising in the Army, which I assured him was not my reason. At Whitehall they were unwilling to have it known that he was dangerously ill, yet in the end they needed to make it known, for he had publicly to name his successor. He named his son, Richard, then, about two in the afternoon, died.

> **RUNNING THE COUNTRY**
> The sorts of government when England had no king were:
> **The Commonwealth, 1649–53.**
> **The Rump,** that part of the Long Parliament that was left after it was weeded out by the Army 1648, ruled first. It made England a republic. This was the Parliament that Cromwell ended in 1653 by thowing them out.
> **Barebones Parliament, 1653**
> Cromwell and the Army still wanted a republic. So elections were held for a new Parliament to run the country as a republic. They had MPs who were nominated rather than properly elected, to make sure they had the 'right' ideas. But there were still too many extreme MPs, so the moderate MPs arranged a vote to give power back to Cromwell.
> **The Protectorate, 1653–9**
> The idea of a republic did not seem to be working. Cromwell and the Army set up a system with 'a single person', but not a king, ruling with Parliament. It was the King of limited monarchy that had been offered to Charles I and refused.
>
> **Ludlow's views**
> Ludlow's views are at their most biased when he discusses the changes to the running of the country. His version of events is changed by his beliefs, especially by his dislike of Cromwell.

CHAPTER 10

Monarchy Restored

Cromwell's death had different effects on the country. Those who had shared his power were troubled, those who had not were glad. Richard Cromwell was now proclaimed Lord Protector, with very little show of joy. One of the first acts of the new government was to arrange the funeral of Oliver Cromwell, which was done with great ceremony. It was decided to call a so-called 'Parliament'. The Council met to decide how to do this. They held elections for a House of Commons and a House of Lords which they filled as best they could with men who depended on them for favours. Not everyone was their creature, for I was elected, yet found I could not sit in the House unless I swore an oath of loyalty to the new Protector, which I was unwilling to do. I got in anyway, but was noticed, and there was a debate about my sitting, or any other, without taking the oath. We were left to sit, but things soon became contentious between those of us who were supporters of the Commonwealth, and the Court party, who wanted nothing but to forward the rule of the new Protector. The Army became involved in the disputes too, especially against the Other House; and wanted to place constraints on the power of the Protector. They mutinied, and all was confusion about how things would be run.

At last it was agreed that the Long Parliament should be restored, to run the country without a Lord Protector. The Parliament chose a new Council of State, that had to swear to be true to the Commonwealth and not accept Charles Stuart, or any other single person, as head. So things went on, yet the Army wanted to have too much of a say in the workings of Parliament. I was, in July, 1659, once more sent to Ireland, this time as Commander-in-Chief. I resolved not to be banished there as I had been by Cromwell, but to return as soon as I could settle matters there. There was much debate as to how the country should be run. Parliament and the Army came into open conflict, and it seemed as though the country would never be settled.

A painting of the coronation procession of Charles II going from the Tower of London to Westminster. It was painted by Dirck Stoop in 1661. Many of the large paintings which tell a story or show an historic occasion were painted by Dutch artists. English artists seem to have concentrated more on portraits. Charles II is the man on the white horse.

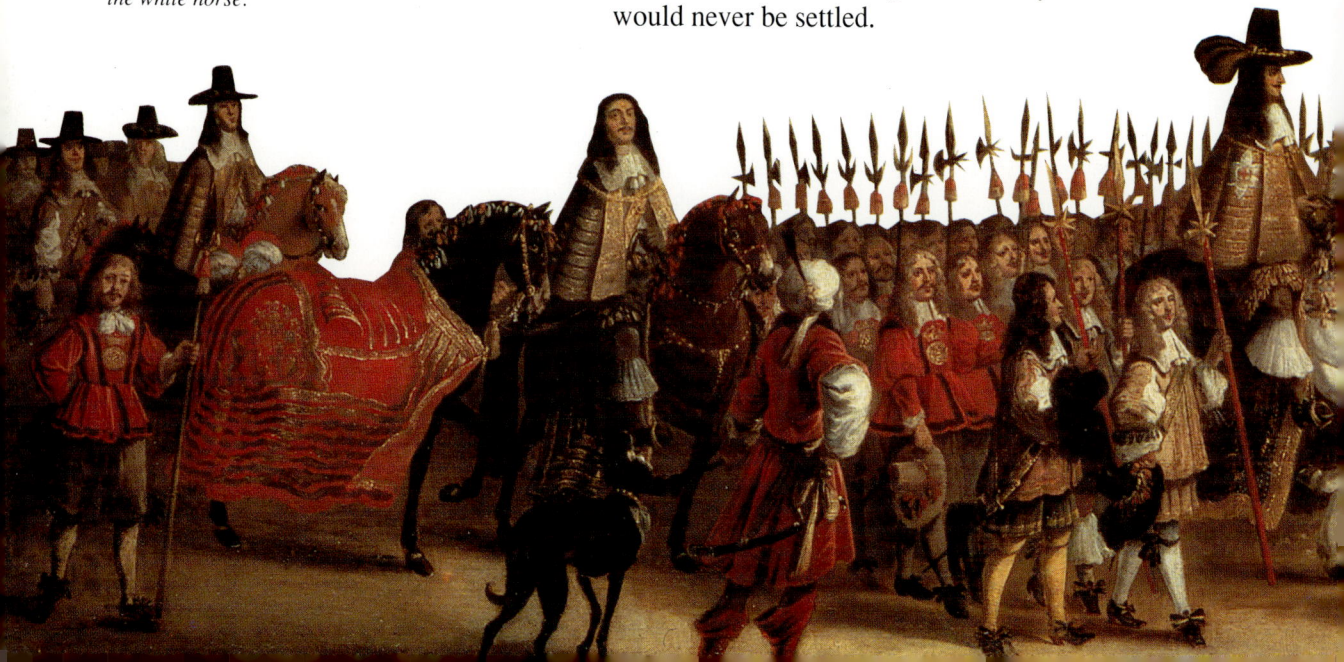

I felt that a breach between Parliament and the Army would prove the ruin of both. I returned to England, to be met with a letter to say that the Army was talking of running the country themselves. By the time I reached Coventry I heard that Colonel Monk, the head of the army in Scotland, had declared himself against this move of the Army. In London I met Fleetwood and said plainly that Monk's declaration seemed better than their demand – government by the sword. Parliament and the Army remained severely at odds. Now Monk resolved to march for London with his army. The Army party gathered their troops together to fight him, and I felt obliged to protest at their actions. I even went to Sir Arthur Hazilrigg to try to persuade him of the need to lay aside animosities and unite our whole strength to keep the Commonwealth from sinking. There were negotiations, to which I was not invited, which reached a settlement. Then the Army decided on a new Parliament, which I argued against, as they had no right to stop the old one. Parliament and the Army were at odds again, and the Royalist party did all they could to further this. Things came to such a pass that I was even accused of treason, but the charges were left. Monk now lost patience with matters in London, and marched on the city. I spoke with him, and he seemed all in favour of a Commonwealth. He spent some time in London, trying to get an agreement with all parties. He continued to make solemn protestations of his being against a King and a House of Lords. Now, with a new militia and a so-called Parliament, he called for the Lords who had sat in 1648, to sit again. Charles Stuart, eldest son of the late King, hearing of this, left the Spanish territories he had then lived in and went to Breda, in the Netherlands, where the House of Commons voted 'That the government of the nation should be by a King, Lords and Commons, and that Charles Stuart should be made King of England'. And so, on 8 May, 1660, the proclamation was made public and the King invited to return.

ANY KING WILL DO?

It was said at the time that the English were only comfortable with a king-like figure at the head of the government. Certainly there is an interesting comparison between reactions to the accession of Richard Cromwell (the new Lord Protector, son of Oliver Cromwell) in 1658 and the accession of Charles II in 1660.

Richard Cromwell
There were loud cries of 'God save the Lord Protector' and great applause. In some parts free wine and beer were given out, guns were fired, bells were rung and bonfires lit.

Charles II
The people celebrated the accession of the new king with drinking, bonfires (some with dummies of Oliver Cromwell on the top), bell ringing and gunfire.

Chapter 11

Royalist Revenge

I now tried to re-enter the House of Commons, and this I did, despite the fact that there were some who wished to see me imprisoned or worse. The King's party were in control here now, and passed a resolution to imprison everyone who had signed the late King's death warrant. Although this motion was made in secret, yet I was told of it, so I went to stay with friends and waited for further news. I heard that the lands of these men were also to be taken, which was against the law to do such a thing before trial or conviction. This was set before the King even arrived from Holland. He came, and confirmed all that had been done, and an order was sent for us to surrender. I did not know what to do. My wife went about asking advice of many – some advised me to surrender, in the hopes of clemency; others advised me to flee. At last I went to the House and gave myself up, and was allowed to return to my lodgings having given them **security**. Yet I was uneasy, for a friend of mine heard Monk tell the King that there was not a man in the country more violently against him, or more dangerous to his interests than I was. The debates in Parliament about how to deal with us went on, and the Lords suggested all should lose their lands, but only some, who they listed, should be beheaded. The Commons argued about the exceptions, and I was now unsure if I was **exempted** or not. Beheading began, including that of Sir John Bouchier. I was advised that if I now went to the Tower I would be exempted, but if I did not, I would die. Yet I was also advised that if I stayed I was lost. Sir Henry Vane was cited as one who had done all that was asked, yet was not exempt. I resolved to go.

I settled my affairs, took leave of my dearest friends and relations, and made my way to Lewes, with some others, avoiding all towns where we suspected there might be soldiers. The next morning we set sail, and reached Dieppe by evening, where I was offered lodgings in Dieppe or in the country. I chose the latter, to be able to walk about without being recognized, Dieppe being at that time full of Irish, who might recognize me. Some days later I had letters with a proclamation about me, requiring people to sieze my person, with the sum of £300 as a reward for this. The letters desired me to remove myself to some place more distant from England. So I said goodbye to the family who had looked after me so well, and set out for Geneva, by way of Rouen, and Paris. In Paris I spent some days viewing such things as were said to be worth seeing. The Louvre seemed more like a garrison than a court, being full of soldiers and dirt. I got more pleasure in seeing the King's horses than I would have had in seeing their master, who treats them better than his miserable people. At Geneva I lodged with a M. Perrot, who fought in our army, and understood the English tongue. His wife was English, so I found her beer good after the fatigue of my journey and constant drinking of wine, which was bad for me.

> **LUDLOW'S LAST YEARS**
>
> Ludlow stayed in Vevay and very little is known of him, with one exception. In 1688, when William and Mary came to the throne, he returned to England 'hoping to be of some public service'. He arrived in England in August 1689. While his friends were glad to see him, there were very few others who wanted to have one of the 'regicides' (those who had signed the death warrant of Charles I) in England. There was a debate in Parliament suggesting that he should be arrested. It seems as though no one spoke in his defence. He returned to Vevay. He died in 1692.
>
> His wife, who had joined him in Vevay in 1663, had returned to England by 1694, and died in 1702.

Letters arrived, to say there were various rumours circulating about me – some said I had been taken while trying to escape in disguise, others that I was in hiding in England. Letters came regularly with news from England. I heard of the executions of my friends, the disbanding of the army, the confiscation of my lands, even of plots I was said to be making to march on London. Searches were made for me which caused trouble to my friends and to my wife, their homes and their persons were searched over and over to find either myself or letters from me.

I was not the only exile in Geneva and now it was suggested that we should publicly ask the city for protection. As this had been privately promised, I did not see the need. I thought it would be dangerous in advertising our whereabouts and would put the city in danger on our account. Yet the request was made and, seeing the city hesitate, we also applied to Berne for protection, which was quickly granted. So we moved to Lausanne, where more exiles joined us in September and October 1662. We were then advised to move to the town of Vevay, which we did. Here we were received with Members of the Council said they would help us all they could. We then received word that there were plots against us, and that one Riardo had been sent to assassinate as many of us as he could. On Sunday, 15 November, 1663, our landlord, going to church early, saw a boat by the lake with persons sitting with cloaks around them near the way. He concluded that they had weapons under their cloaks, and were waiting to waylay us on our way to church, so kept them from us. We were advised to leave, but I feared we would make matters worse by going to a place where we were not known and losing the friends we had. Instead we strengthened our house with the help of the town, and things were arranged so that I could ring the alarm bell from the house itself. We were also brought news from our friends in the village of any suspicious persons in the area – for some came as sailors on the lake, others as grooms looking for work – so we could be better on our guard. Indeed, the people of the town helped us foil any attempt on our lives, so we resolved to stay where people were so well disposed towards us.

One of the two prints of Edmund Ludlow that are known to exist. He does not seem to have had an oil painting made of himself at around this time, unlike almost every other military commander. This print was made after his death and shows him in the dress of the late seventeenth century.

Glossary

All definitions refer to Ludlow's use of the word in the 1600s.

Army this is used to refer to the New Model Army (see box on page 29) which, because of its success and Parliament's dependence on it, became a political power in England.

arbitrary without reference to anyone else.

artillery cannon of various sizes.

body a large group of people, all together.

breach a large hole in something like a wall or a dam.

case-shot a tin container, filed with musket balls, which was designed to burst on impact.

colour another name for a standard (*see* **standard**). It was sometimes used to refer to sashes of certain colours used by both sides in the Civil Wars to identify regiments.

commonwealth the people and the country of England.

Commonwealth the government of England in the 1650s when used with a capital 'C'.

contrivance making something you want happen.

dragoons soldiers who were armed with muskets and rode horses but dismounted to fight.

engaged in the sense that Ludlow uses it in describing battles, this means fighting with the enemy.

field pieces cannons. All were big enough to need to be mounted on wheels and fired by more than one man.

foot soldiers who fought on foot, as opposed to soldiers who fought on horseback. There were two sorts of foot soldiers: pikemen (*see* **pikemen**) and musketeers (*see* **musketeers**).

gangrene an infection that often developed in wounds at the time, because no one knew about germs and infection. Wounds were seldom properly cleaned, so the infection made the flesh rot. The only solution was to cut off the affected part of the body, if possible.

garrison a group of soldiers left to guard a place.

great shot cannon balls.

gun cannon, *not* pistols or hand-held weapons.

horse soldiers who fought on horseback.

leads strips of lead, used to cover a roof.

match a long fuse, made of thin rope, which was carried by a musketeer. He used it to fire his musket.

militia an army of citizens rather than trained soldiers. Men were organized into militia bands that were supposed to train regularly, in case they were needed to fight an invasion. Few people took this training seriously.

minister another name for a priest or clergyman.

musket an early sort of hand-gun, between 1.25 and 1.5 metres long.

musketeers   soldiers who fought on foot firing muskets at the enemy. They could harm the enemy from further away than pikemen, but muskets took a long time to load and fire.

muster   soldiers gathering together for inspection.

nail   cannons were put out of action by jamming a piece of metal (like a nail) in the hole used to light the gunpowder.

outhouses   building around the edge of castle wall, mostly used to store things and animals.

parley   a meeting between opposing groups, under truce, to talk.

party   a group of people.

pikemen   footsoldiers who fought with swords and pikes. Pikes were long spear-like weapons. They were supposed to be 6 metres long. This made them very heavy and hard to carry and use. Many pikemen cut the end of their pikes off, to make them closer to 4 metres in length.

poison   cannons were poisoned by putting things down the barrel so that the cannon ball stuck in the barrel. This meant that the gunpowder could not fire the cannon ball when it was lit. Instead, it exploded in the cannon, sometimes blowing the cannon to pieces, always ruining it.

quartered   found somewhere to eat and sleep.

relieved   either saved from the enemy altogether, or brought supplies of food and ammunition to keep a siege going.

routed   driven away.

sacrament   one of the key religious rights of the Christian churches. In this case, Ludlow is referring to Holy Communion, which was administered to Charles I by William Juxton, Bishop of London, on the morning of his execution.

scouts   one or more people sent out to find out what is ahead, or what the movements of the enemy are.

security   a promise to do something or lose money or land, depending on what is agreed.

slight   to damage the defences of a castle or a town so the enemy cannot use it.

standard   a flag that has a symbol on it to show what army group it represents. (See picture on page 31.)

storm   to attack suddenly and take by force.

terms   conditions agreed before something is done.

truce   a pause in fighting, agreed by both sides, but not the end of the war.

undermine   to dig a tunnel under a wall, to blow up gunpowder in it and knock the wall down.

usurpation   taking over illegally.

wheel about   this command meant that the soldiers should turn around to face the other way.

wheel-locks   a sort of pistol. (See box on page 19.)

wing   one side of an army. Horse were placed on both wings of an army. They were supposed to swing round and hit the enemy hard and fast from the side, drive through them, then attack from behind.

Index

Numbers in *italic* type refer to captions; numbers in **bold** type refer to information boxes.

animals, cattle 15
    horses 9, 12, 15, 16, *24*, 25, *27*
armies, confusion in battle 11, **11**
    fighting (see fighting)
    New Model 28, **29**, **30**
    Parliamentarian 6, 8, 10, 11, 12, 13, 14, 15
    payment 11, 15, 16, 18, 25
    Royalist 8, 9, 10, 11, 12, 13, 14, 16
armour 7, 8–9, *10*, *12*, 28, 29, 34, *45*

battles, Brentford 13
    Edgehill 10–11, *13*
    Newbury (Second) 26–7
    Powicke Bridge 8
    Preston **33**
    Turnham Green 14
Bradshaw, Sergeant John 34, *34*, 35, 36

Charles I 6, 7, *7*, 14, *14*, 18, 23, **24**, 27, 30, 31
    character **7**, 13, 23, 33, 35, **35**
    negotiations with his enemies (see negotiations)
    on the Isle of Wight 32, *32*, 33
    trial and execution 34–7, *37*
Charles II *42–3*, 43, **43**
communications, messages 12, 45
    passwords **11**
    rumours 8
    signals 41
Cromwell, Oliver **9**, 38, 39, 40, *40*, 41
Cromwell, Richard 42, **43**

doctors (see wounds and sickness)

Essex, Earl of 7, 9, 11, 14, 23, 24, **25**
exile, attempts to assassinate during 45
    Ludlow forced into 44
    reward offered for Ludlow during 44

fighting 7, 8, 9, 10, *11*, 25
    conditions 9, 10, 11, 12, *27*, 29
    experience 8, 9, **9**
    mistakes 11, 12, 14, 24
    tactics 7, 10, 12, 13, *13*, 14, 24, *24*, 25, 28
    training 6, **9**, *24*
    weapons (see weapons)

Independents 30, 32, **33**

Inns of Court 5, 6
Instrument of Government 40, 41
Ireland, Ludlow in 38–9, 40
    relations with England **38**, 39, 42

Levellers **33**
Ludlow, Gabriel 19, 21, 26, **26**

negotiations, between Charles I and Parliament 30, 32, 33
    between Charles I and the Army 32, 33
    between Charles I and the Scots 30, 32, 33
    over capture of Wardour Castle 15
    over surrender of Wardour Castle 17, 18, 19
newspapers *13*, *15*

Oxford 5, 13, 14, *14*, 21, **22**, 23, 24, 27

Parliament **7**, 9, 13, 14, 30, **30**, 31, 32
    elections 39, 40, 41, 42
    Ludlow in 30, 34, 40, 42, 43, 44
    rule without a king 37, 39, *39*, 40–1, 42
Presbyterians **30**, **33**
prisoners 8, 12, 13, 22, *22*, 23, 29
provisions **16**, 25
    camps and quarters 8, 12, 13
    capture of enemy weapons 11, 12, 15
    food and drink 12, 16, **16**, 17, 20

sabotage 16
Scots **24**, 30, 32, 33
scouts 9
servants 11, 12
sieges 15, 15–21, 24, 25, 27, *27*, 28, 29
    mining during 15, 17, 18
    sorties 15, 16, 18
standards *8*, 11, *27*, *31*

towns 23, 25, 27, *27*, 29

Vevay **44**, 45

Waller, Sir William 18, 21, 24, **25**, 26, 27
weapons, ammunition 11
    armour (see armour)
    cannon *8*, 10, 11, 26
    hand guns 18, **19**, *24*
    muskets 7, *8*, *12*, 27
    pikes *8*, *10*, 27
    swords 7, 8
winter 14, **14**, 27
wounds and sickness 16, 18, 19, 20, 26, **26**, 29, 38

48